The House on School Street

Amy and Oliver Ferris with the author
in front of the house on School Street. 1947.

for Andrea
& Dan
♡ Meg

The House on School Street

Eight Generations.
Two Hundred and Four Years. One Family.

MEG FERRIS KENAGY

Meg Ferris Kenagy

Contact: www.megkenagy.com
Portland, Oregon

ISBN 978-1-7321884-0-2

This book is a memoir and a research project. I have endeavored to tell an accurate story, but I assume no responsibility for errors or omissions. Memory, of course, has its own story to tell and mine may not be the same as that of others.

Cover design by Michael Arthur, Michael Arthur Creative Communications, www.macreativeco.com
Cover photo courtesy of the Hingham Historical Society. Martha and Sarah Litchfield in front of the house at 74 School Street. Circa 1890.
Interior design and production by Jennifer Omner, ALL Publications, www.allpublications.com

For my family

Contents

This is a story about a house and a family. It begins in 1785 when a veteran of the Revolutionary War builds the house in which eight generations of my family will live. It travels more than 200 years until my paternal grandmother, the last matriarch, draws her last breath under its roof.

It is a sparse story, based on whispers of story, because the people who live in the house are farmers, firefighters, butchers, carpenters, housewives, and seamstresses who live largely unrecorded lives. There is a magistrate, a deacon, a nurse, and a librarian. There are soldiers, shoemakers, and blacksmiths. They are all immigrants or descended from immigrants. So while it is an American story, it is only a slice of American history. It begins after the arrowheads of the Native Americans have been trodden into this particular piece of ground. It ends before the communications and transportation revolutions rip the world open so that one day, there will be no old families in the village. The houses will be there, but the old families will be gone.

It is the memoir of a house and the people who lived in it. It is a personal story, a work based on years of research, a lengthy trek through land records, wills, photographs, letters, libraries, and history books, but speculation enters. Facts, dates, articles, and legal documents report what the ancestors did; historic events give context to their lives, and occasionally the thread of conjecture stitches a story. All history is, of course, a retelling.

Why I am compelled to tell this story is part of the story. It is not a yearning for times past or an idealization of the small town—as a teenager, I couldn't wait to get out of that small town—but it is my beginning and it stays with me. It is home. Where all our stories begin.

The Family

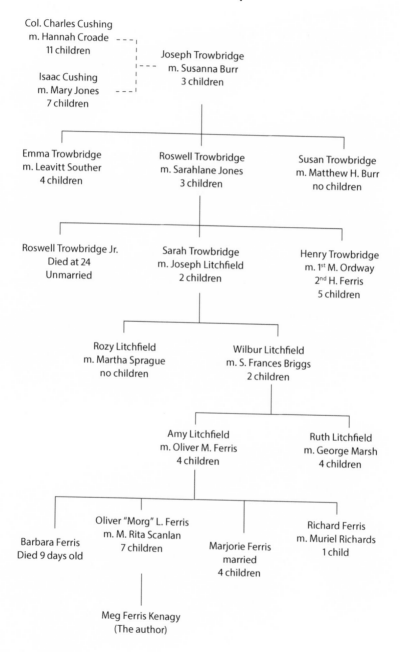

Col. Charles Cushing
m. Hannah Croade
11 children

Isaac Cushing
m. Mary Jones
7 children

Joseph Trowbridge
m. Susanna Burr
3 children

Emma Trowbridge
m. Leavitt Souther
4 children

Roswell Trowbridge
m. Sarahlane Jones
3 children

Susan Trowbridge
m. Matthew H. Burr
no children

Roswell Trowbridge Jr.
Died at 24
Unmarried

Sarah Trowbridge
m. Joseph Litchfield
2 children

Henry Trowbridge
m. 1st M. Ordway
2nd H. Ferris
5 children

Rozy Litchfield
m. Martha Sprague
no children

Wilbur Litchfield
m. S. Frances Briggs
2 children

Amy Litchfield
m. Oliver M. Ferris
4 children

Ruth Litchfield
m. George Marsh
4 children

Barbara Ferris
Died 9 days old

Oliver "Morg" L. Ferris
m. M. Rita Scanlan
7 children

Marjorie Ferris
married
4 children

Richard Ferris
m. Muriel Richards
1 child

Meg Ferris Kenagy
(The author)

The house on School Street 1897.

Chapter 1

The Ancestors

Home is a name, a word, it is a strong one;
stronger than magician ever spoke, or spirit ever
answered to, in the strongest conjuration.

—Charles Dickens

They are there before I am, and they have been there a long time. They are there in a dry old book left open, in the creak of the spinning wheel in the attic, in the whoosh of the fire coming alive on the grate. They are there in the birds that sweep low over the garden, my grandmother saying their names—*black-capped chickadee, bluebird, purple finch, sparrow*—with barely a glance.

"Oh, comings and goings," my grandmother says when I hear something upstairs or in another room of the dimly lit old house. And they are that, comings and goings. There is the sense of coming into a room when someone is leaving, a rustle and a draft on the stairs, a banging screen door, a shadow across the window.

And in that same garden on summer days, women in long white dresses bend down to pluck an iris or cut a rose only to fade away. Are they there on the hot waves of sunlight, or do I imagine them? And the woman who comes to me many years later in a dream, who is she? She sits, the dream woman, in the large bed in the back upstairs room of the old house on School Street. She looks out the window, watching blackbirds drift across the sky. I see what she sees: a split-rail fence, a field of gold hay. I listen with her, leaning into the house, which is dead quiet. We watch dust motes dance in the stream of sunlight that makes pale yellow rectangles on the floor. We wait for someone. She folds her hands over her pregnant belly. We strain to hear through the thick silence in the house, and the silence goes on and on until she fades. It is a dream where nothing happens, where nothing moves but birds and dust. A dream that won't leave me, because it is real, and because it is wrong. I know well enough the room and the window, but when I was a child, there was no such landscape. When I looked out that window, I saw a thicket of apple, maple, and fir trees and a clothesline. There was no fence. There were no hay fields or any long view. That view, I learned later, had been gone for decades.

So I could say it was the women in the garden or the whispers too thin to be deciphered or the posy of flowers left in a cemetery. I could say it was the fullness of an empty room or the comings and goings in the old house on School Street that grew into my fascination with the lives of the seven generations of my family who lived in the house before me. Because I am of the eighth generation, and I always felt, I always thought, somehow they were still there.

Chapter 2

The Eighth Generation, 1946

Time flies over us, but leaves its shadow behind.

—Nathaniel Hawthorne

I am born into the past in a small town on the northeastern seaboard. It is a fall day with a deep chill. There is the taste of salt on the restless little west wind that rattles the remnant leaves that cling to the maple trees. As the sun rises, it illuminates the rocky, forested landscape. It reflects off the harbor and the white church spires and the river that rises in a meeting of waters and meanders across the town to the rich broth of its estuary. Ponds light up like pocket mirrors as the sun moves higher in the sky and the frost on the windows of the family homestead on School Street turns to rivulets of water.

Cast the die. I am born on my mother's birthday, sun in Scorpio, moon in Leo on a day shorter than its night. Years later, the astrologer who reads my natal chart tells me that at the time of my birth, it is growing dark. The sun is setting. Mercury is setting. Mars is setting. Venus is setting. The moon has set. The moon is, in fact, at its lower culmination in the fourth house— the position associated with family, ancestry, and heritage.

"Family issues in this chart," she says, "are monumental."

This is not what I had hoped to hear when I consulted the astrologer.

————•◦•————

My mother wakes early that November day in the cold upstairs bedroom in the house on School Street. The ancient fireplace is no longer in use, and ice crystals have painted delicate patterns on the windowpanes. The furnace in the cellar blows heat into the downstairs rooms, but no warmth makes its way up the stairs. My mother is not used to the cold of an unheated house, and she has unpacked all the quilts from her hope chest. "They didn't have much on School Street," she says. "No one had much." The depression, war years, and rationing have taken a toll—things are used up, worn out. Towels are frayed, sheets are thin, clothes mended and remade. Tires, if you have a car, are patched and repatched. If not, you might use a bit of rubber to cover the hole in your shoe. Nothing is thrown away, because replacing anything is hard.

They take the narrow back stairs to the first floor. My father knocks on his parents' bedroom door to tell them he is taking my mother to the hospital. He has a car, a Ford. My grandmother follows them out into the frosty side yard and stands there in her thin cotton housecoat, waving until they are out of sight.

I am two weeks overdue, but my mother claims she is in no hurry to deliver. When I wasn't born on her due date, she tells me, "Everyone said maybe I should just wait and have the baby on my birthday, and I thought that would be nice because Daddy came home from the war on my birthday the year before."

"Daddy" is my father. "Home" is Hingham, Massachusetts. And, although the Second World War had effectively ended in August 1945 when Fat Boy and Little Man were dropped on Japan, my father did not ship out of Saipan until November.

"He promised me he'd be home on my birthday, and I thought he would be," my mother says. "So I stayed up until midnight." There is no call. Disappointed, she goes to bed. At 3 a.m., the heavy black phone on the telephone table in the front hall rings. My father has landed in San Francisco and raced for a phone booth.

"It was just midnight in California, still my birthday," she says, pleasure creeping into her voice after all the years.

The call makes the rest of the wait bearable. From San Francisco, my father is transported to Fort Devens where, on November 23, 1945, he is discharged from the United States Army and shuttled aboard a train to Boston. My mother and his brother Richard are at North Station to meet him.

"He was carrying a pack as big as he was," my mother remembers. He also carried a Victory Medal, a Good Conduct Medal, an American Pacific Theatre Ribbon, and an Asiatic Pacific Theatre Campaign Ribbon.

From the train station, they go to my father's house on School Street. His parents, grandmother, brother, and sister live there, but they find room for two more, and, in that late November of 1945, my mother and father move into the upstairs northwest chamber and begin to create—I have to believe somewhat tentatively—their life together. They had only been married four days when my father was inducted into the Army. He was gone for three and a half years.

You can see in their early photos that my mother is beautiful and my father handsome. In this one, they sit on the steps of the hotel in New Hampshire where they honeymooned. Her white puff-sleeved blouse is tucked into a pair of fashionable wide-leg trousers. My father, his arm around her tiny waist, wears a white long-sleeved shirt, striped tie, and suspenders. Then, here he is in his uniform, standing in the front yard on School Street with his mother and grandmother. He is leaving this day. He will soon be in Oakland, California, then in Hawaii, and then on the island of Guam—exotic places none of them have been or will ever be.

———————◆◆———————

My mother and I spend nine days in the hospital, an average amount of time in 1946. She makes friends with everyone on the maternity ward. She is social, my mother. My father comes after work and looks at me from behind a wall of glass. And when we come home it is to family. There is nowhere else to go. The housing shortage is acute. Millions of returning soldiers are looking for a place to live. We stay for a time on School Street and for a time with my mother's parents in Dorchester; that house is also overflowing.

Fortune in the form of the government intervenes. We qualify for a two-bedroom apartment in the Hingham Naval barracks, which have been converted into housing for veterans. Our apartment rents for $32 a month. We are lucky says my Yankee father; we are blessed says my Irish mother. In this place I learn to climb stairs and ride a tricycle. I play in a sandbox with a boy named Sonny. I watch a record spin on a hi-fi music player. I meet snow. My mother laughs. I get a baby sister and, while my mother is in the hospital, I am sent for two weeks to my grandparents' house on School Street where my grandmother and great-grandmother spoil me.

In 1949 my parents buy a house. Late in his life, my father remembers every detail. "We looked at a house for sale in Hingham Centre near my mother's house. It was small and had no cellar and no central heat. But we liked it and bought it for $4,500 with a 4½ percent mortgage for 20 years." He digs a cellar, adds rooms, and enlarges the lean-to bathroom. The rooms are necessary because by 1956, I have six younger sisters: Ann, Judy, Susan, Mary, and the twins, Ellen and Amy.

This crowded chaotic household is home, but I love any time spent with my grandmother in the old house. Here, quiet routines turn the day and the year as they have for generations. We shake clothes from a basket and pin them on the line with wood clothespins. We pick vegetables and pull weeds. We rake leaves and walk in the snow; I run ahead and back, melting snowflakes on my tongue. We take flowers to the cemetery, which is just down the street. We go to the library. At night, we sleep in high beds with our books. Bedside lamps make puddles of light in the dark. When I am older, I sleep in the four-poster bed in the upstairs back bedroom, the bed of the unknown woman I will dream about many years later.

There is no car at my grandparents' house. Two ruts in the grass in the side yard serve as a driveway for visitors. The house smells of dry wood and dust. Fires burn in the downstairs fireplaces. We wear sweaters. The wind rattles the windows. My grandmother knits. My grandfather reads his newspaper. There is a radio that crackles in the evening, and there is a puzzle table. My great-grandmother Frances lives upstairs. I can go up and play cards with her—crazy eights, go fish, slap jack—before she takes her long white hair down and makes it into a braid and goes to bed. When it is late, the house creaks and pops. The pipes bang, that's what my grandmother says. The house whispers and people come and go in and out of rooms. I am young. I don't know who is who. Still, there is something here that I don't understand. It's not like my other house.

———————◆•——————

It will be years before I turn my gaze to the past with any intensity. My children will be grown, my grandmother dead, my parents dead. It will be years before I wonder why my early memories of the house on School Street linger. It will be years before I accept what the astrologer told me—that at the time of my birth, it was growing dark. That the sun was setting. That Mercury was setting. That Mars was setting. That Venus was setting. That the moon had set. That the moon was in the fourth house—the house of home. That the die *was* cast.

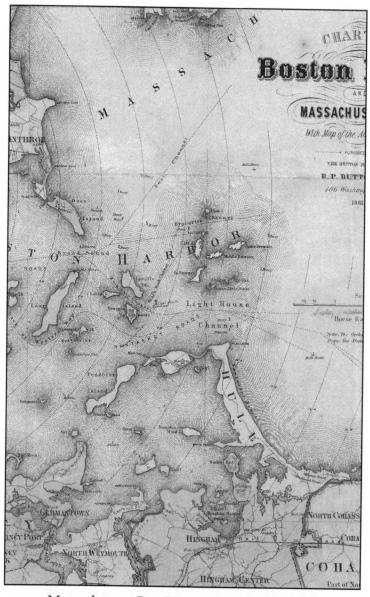

Massachusetts Bay. Hingham, its harbor, and
the Centre are at the bottom of the map.

Chapter 3

Colonel Charles Cushing
The First Owner, 1785

*Capt. Charles Cushing was a descendant of one of the first
settlers of Hingham. Besides efficient military service in the
Revolution, he held many civil offices, and represented the town
in both the House and the Senate. He was known later in life
as Colonel Cushing. His home was at Hingham Centre.*

—*History of the Town of Hingham, Massachusetts*

There is a small plaque on the front corner of my grandparents'
house on School Street that reads "Col. Charles Cushing House,
Built 1785," but I never wonder who Charles Cushing is and how
I am related to him until anyone in the family who would have
known is long dead. Eventually, I learn the answer. Matthew
Cushing who came to the town from Hingham, England in 1638
is our common ancestor. But that is well in the future after—
like Alice down the rabbit hole—I have fallen headlong into the
past.

It is 1785. The war has been over for two years. Colonel Cushing is building a house in Hingham Centre, one of a handful of small villages that make up the town of 2,000. He and his brothers are awash in land. Their parents died during the war years, and they have inherited a great deal of property. He chooses a five-acre parcel on the river, a stone's throw from the paternal homestead where his brothers live. He situates the house at the front of the lot, facing the narrow dirt road. The lion's share of land is behind it and to the north. Like much of the town's land, it has been cleared for farming, stripped of shrubs, trees, and rocks. Local builders are hired. Huge timber frames are built and, on one clear day, "the house and barns were raised." Carpenters and masons build the massive central chimney with its five fireplaces and lay the wide-plank pine floors. The roof is framed, boarded, and shingled, and the house is finished before winter.

From the front, it looks like a house a child might draw—a two-story rectangle with a big chimney in the center of the roof. There are two windows on each side of the front door and five windows on the second floor. It is an impressive house built by a prosperous man. But it is not pretentious and, as use defines it, it is a farmhouse. The only embellishment is the paneled front door, which is flanked by pilasters and topped with a pediment in a Georgian flourish.

The door opens into a central hall; the staircase is directly ahead. A door to the right leads to the parlor, a door to the left to the dining room. Both of these rooms open directly into the two back rooms; the parlor leads to the Colonel's office, and the dining room leads to the kitchen. At the north end of the kitchen is a narrow birthing room. Upstairs, the two front rooms overlook the road, and the two back rooms face the river. One of the back rooms is actually a large hall with two sets of stairs, one leads to the first floor, the other to the attic. Outdoors there are an outhouse, hennery, and barn. Fences are built and a lean-to pantry is added off the kitchen.

This house will survive for more than 200 years. Here, babies will be born, young and old will die, men will leave for war, love will be made and lost, and one day, I will watch television, jump on the big beds, and play hide-and-go-seek. Of course, in 1785 this cannot be imagined. Things are in disarray, a war has been won, but the country has yet to adopt a constitution or elect a president. Daily life on a farm is not easy. A house is a place to live, to shelter, while work is done and children are raised.

———◆◆———

Charles Cushing is born in 1744 in Hingham Centre into an accomplished family, one of the first political dynasties in America—they are politicians, lawyers, military leaders, and judges. Charles' father, Jacob, is a Harvard man, a judge, and a legislator. His mother, Mary Chauncy, is a child of Boston's elite Puritan class. Her father was a merchant, her grandfather a minister, and her great-grandfather the second president of Harvard College. So it is in a meeting of prestigious families that Jacob Cushing and Mary Chauncy marry in Boston in the winter of 1739. If the harbor isn't clogged with ice, they return to Hingham by boat, sailing past the small rocky islands, arriving at the dock while it is still daylight. A horse and buggy takes them through the cluster of shops that surround the harbor, up Main Street past the Meetinghouse of the First Parish, and over Pear Tree Hill into the village of Hingham Centre. It is just over a mile from the harbor, but to Mary, it is another world, a long way from the bustle of Boston. Here is where they start their life together and where their three sons, Jacob Jr., Charles, and Isaac are born.

The boys are baptized in the church—their mother's family is of the "most religious Puritan stamp"—and in their father's politics. They are educated well. Their father is active in the fight for independence, and all three of them will serve in the Revolution when it comes. And, like their father, all of them will farm. Jacob Jr. makes it his primary business, Charles follows his father into the law, and Isaac becomes a sawmill owner and a deacon of the First Parish. We are interested in Charles, of course, because he builds the house, but we are also interested in Isaac, because one day, he will buy it from his brother.

When he is twenty-four, Charles, the "Colonel" as he comes to be known, marries twenty-one-year-old Hannah Croade from the nearby town of Halifax. There is no mystery as to how they met. She is his first cousin. Her mother and his father are sister and brother.

Hannah, the fifteenth of Thomas and Rachel Croade's sixteen children, is born in the summer of 1747. Thomas, a merchant and founding member of the church, is one of Halifax's leading citizens. He owns a large farm and several slaves. He is also a magistrate who is remembered, in part, for the "elegant" handwriting with which he records the town registry. His wife Rachel is remembered, in the aggregate, for being the mother of his sixteen children and dying in her forty-ninth year. When she is buried in December 1753, Hannah is only six years old. Her sisters raise her until their father remarries.

The Croade household is a busy one, but one less crowded than it might have been, because many of Hannah's siblings die young. In fact, five of the couple's first six children died as infants. They are buried, three boys and two girls, in the old cemetery, winged skulls engraved on their headstones. Why they die is undocumented, but prematurity and infectious disease take many young lives in the eighteenth century. The death of a child is a great grief, intensely suffered, but it is not uncommon. It is God's will, so the mother goes on to have more children, increasing her own risk of death with each pregnancy.

The Colonel and Hannah marry on February 23, 1769 at the Croade family farm. They live for a time in her father's house but are soon in Hingham where they start their family. As a wife, Hannah now has a place in the community and the church—they belong to the First Parish, the original Puritan church, where the Colonel holds a pew—but her life will be lived at home. She will bear eleven children, the first when she is twenty-two, the last when she is forty-five, and her days will be measured by how soon after their births she returns to her kitchen.

On the morning of April 19, 1775, an alarm rider flies into Hingham Square, his horse's hooves kicking up dust. His cry, "To arms!" "To arms!," is not heard in the Centre, but the tolling of the Meetinghouse bell carries over the hill, and suddenly, the whole town is in motion. Men pick up muskets and ammunition. Teenagers reach for their drums and look to their mothers for breakfast. Knapsacks are stuffed with clothes, pencils, soap, and stockings. Hannah says good-bye to her husband at the door or in the kitchen, a baby in her arms and three at her skirt. The Colonel and his brothers report to the training field. In all, 154 townsmen march to Boston that day, four companies of farmers, fishermen, carpenters, and blacksmiths. Jacob Jr. and the Colonel march with the infantry and Isaac with the artillery.

The war lasts eight years, and the Colonel serves throughout,

coming home between enlistments to check on his family and
businesses. At the beginning of the war, he is in Boston, building
forts and helping to maintain the siege that pins the British Army
within city limits. In the summer, he is promoted to Captain and
stationed in Cambridge, serving under General George Washington who has arrived to take charge of the Continental Army.
Over the winter, the Americans fortify their positions above the
city, moving cannons to high ground. In March, the British, fearing their supply lines will be cut, evacuate, sailing for Canada.

The colonists reoccupy the city and the theater of war shifts.
General Washington takes his army to New York. The Colonel is
sent to Canada in lead of a Hingham Company to reinforce the
troops fighting there. The Canadian Campaign, or Invasion of
Quebec, is one of the first big offensives of the war and one of the
most disastrous. Intended to prevent the British from building
a fighting force in Canada and attacking the colonies from the
north, the mission is not going well. Even as the British pull out
of Boston, the American Army is huddled outside Quebec City,
poorly provisioned and fighting an epidemic of smallpox, a force
that will prove more deadly than the enemy.

The Long War

In June 1776, the Colonel is on the Isle-aux-Noix in the Richelieu
River with the remnant American army, which is in full retreat
from Canada. British ships carrying reinforcements have arrived
in Quebec City with the spring thaw. The American troops, weak
from a frigid winter, lack of food, and disease, have no choice but
to withdraw. Eventually, they end up here, on the Isle-aux-Noix
where they await boats to take them to the American-held fort
at Crown Point in New York. Once there, the Colonel describes
the ordeal in a letter to his brother in Hingham.

... a great part of the Army were sick, many with the small pox, and many of those who had had it were sick with the flux. Here we were obliged to wait for boats eight days, where we could get nothing but pork and flour. The island being small, not more than one mile in length, and a quarter of a mile in width, the land low, the days hot, and at night great dews, and such a number of men on so small a spot, and many of them sick—the place stunk enough to breed an infection.

———————◆◆———————

Several months earlier, the Colonel and his company of Hingham men march to New York. From Albany, they make their way into Canada "in the greatest hurry, passing through great difficulty and fatigue . . . till we came to the mouth of the river Sorel, where, to our great surprise, we heard of the retreat of the army from Quebeck." In Sorel, an American camp on the Lawrence River, they encounter retreating troops, many of them sick with smallpox. "Boat loads sick with it were landed among us, so that there seemed no possibility of escaping it," writes the Colonel. The only hope is inoculation, a practice prohibited by the Army. The rules are strict; it is "Death for any Doctor who attempted Inoculation." The Colonel and several other officers, however, allow their men to inoculate themselves. The decision is the right one and later, while he is helping bury the dead at Crown Point—"some days not less than fifteen or twenty"—he is able to write home that he "led a company of seventy-six men into Canada, and brought them all out." General Washington will eventually reverse his stance on inoculation as a method to prevent smallpox, in part because of the misery and death in Canada, but it comes too late for the Army, which flees Canada in a desperate state.

When the Colonel finally rides into Hingham, he is recovered from smallpox but "sick with fever and ague." He is exhausted and filthy. He has been in the saddle for days, traveling from New York, following the Old Mohawk trail over Hoosac Mountain. It is rugged terrain. Inhospitable country. The historian who reports his journey writes that the Colonel was "the first white man who ever crossed that Mountain."

The Colonel is home, but he is not done with the Continental Army—the war is still in its early days and he will serve again. The Canadian Campaign is behind him, however, as much as it ever will be.

Peace and Politics

The war is over. A peace treaty is signed in Paris. The Americans are victorious, but the tasks before them are monumental. Thirteen colonies must become a united country. A national government, a monetary system, and a stable economy have to be created. The Colonel will dedicate his life to this work, but now, in the aftermath of the war, he will build a house.

The Colonel, Hannah, and their six children—they have buried two—move into the house on School Street in the late summer or fall of 1785. Fires are lit. Pots, dishes, and utensils are unpacked. A heavy pot is hung from the crane in the kitchen fireplace. Water is put on to heat. The scent of baking bread fills the room. The Colonel's desk and bookcase are set down in his office. Beds, chests of drawers, and trunks of clothes are carried up the stairs. All in all, furnishings are sparse.

From the kitchen window, Hannah looks out over barren fields. Wintering robins shelter in the trees that straggle along the fence line, and the big autumn sky weighs heavy on the land. It is a scene that foreshadows a bleak season. On the first day of December, fourteen-year-old Charles Junior dies. No cause of death is recorded.

Hannah is thirty-eight when she buries her son. Thin sunlight offers little comfort. Death has come to the house. A memory lingers. Neighbors visit, prayers are offered, and life goes on. Hannah has other children who need her, and she is pregnant.

The new baby, her ninth, arrives after the spring equinox when the earth is warming and crocuses are pushing through the mud. Someone in the household is sent to fetch the midwife. Hannah's women, her female relatives and neighbors, come with food, herbs, and linens. Water is heated and children fed. God and faith are evoked and, this day, a healthy baby girl is delivered. She is named for her mother. The first baby born in the new house, she will live to be twenty-five.

Hannah will have two more babies, both boys, both named Charles. The first, born in 1789, will live two years. The second, born in 1792, will live four years and ten months.

The Colonel is a town selectman and a member of the school committee. At the state level, he is a representative for eight years and a member of the Senate for one. Then comes the presidential election of 1796. George Washington has refused a third term. The Federalist Party, which calls for a strong national government, has nominated John Adams. The Democratic-Republicans are running Thomas Jefferson. The Colonel is a Republican. Haven't they just fought a war to rid themselves of a strong central government? Didn't he witness the cost of that war and the suffering in Canada?

After Adams wins, the Colonel becomes increasingly annoyed by the political changes in town. Hingham Centre resident Fearing Burr writes in his diary that indeed the Colonel is "so vexed by the Federalists coming into power that he left town," moving his family to Lunenburg in the central part of the state.

Be that as it may, the Colonel and Hannah have other reasons to move to Lunenburg. Several of their children and grandchildren live there, and Hannah would relish the thought of being close to them, but while their furniture and possessions are loaded onto horse-drawn wagons, does she walk one last time through the house? Three of her children were born under its roof. Four of them died while she lived here. Does she reflect on her age that day? She is forty-nine, the same age as her mother when she died. Her childbearing days are over. She will no longer suffer that pain, but she will live a long, long time and suffer many others. In a dozen years, she will bury her husband and, in time, she will bury all but three of her eleven children.

Their Works do Follow Them

The Colonel and Hannah settle on a homestead near the center of town. He dies here at age sixty-five after a long illness, leaving his real estate to Hannah. There is the house and land and half of a pew in the church. There is a long inventory of property, including a desk, bookcase, furniture, quilts, dishes, silver tablespoons, a spinning wheel, tools, a chaise and harness, a saddle and bridle, twenty-five bushels of potatoes, barrels of cider, and much more. But Hannah lives a long time, and her resources dwindle. She moves in with one of her daughters, and on May 1, 1837 she applies to the government for the Colonel's war pension.

It has been a long wait—she is eighty-nine—but legislation has just been passed that allows widows to claim their husbands' military pensions. Hannah is too frail to make the trip to the courthouse, so Judge Solomon Strong of the Court of Common Pleas comes to her home. She testifies that she is "the widow of Charles Cushing," and that they lived in Hingham when he went into service. She provides the letter her husband wrote describing his service in Canada and indicates "the family Bible, belonging to my husband and in which all the family records were kept." She signs the judge's report with an X.

An X. My heart wrenches. Hannah Croade Cushing, daughter of a man recognized for his elegant handwriting, wife of a politician and soldier whose letters inform the history of the Revolution, mother of eleven, could not write her name.

Two weeks later Hannah dies and is buried next to her husband. Today, their weather-worn headstones stand side by side in the North Cemetery in Lunenburg, hand-carved wings and words eroding with every season.

Charles Cushing

Sacred to the memory of Hon. Charles Cushing, Esq., who departed this life, after a lingering and painful disease, which he supported with Christian fortitude and resignation, Nov. 25th, 1809, aet. 65.

He served his country in her contest for the obtainment of freedom and independence, and has since sustained with honor several important offices, both civil and military. He was no less endeared to his family connections by his disposition to disseminate knowledge and promote the social virtues than to the community by his public spirit and charity.

Blessed are the dead who die in the Lord; yea, saith the Spirit, for they rest from their labors, and their works do follow them.

Hannah Cushing

Sacred to the memory of Mrs. Hannah, consort of the late Hon. Charles Cushing who died May 13, 1837; aged 90. Blessed are the dead who die in the Lord.

The First Parish Meetinghouse, the Old Ship,
was built in the summer of 1681.

Chapter 4

Deacon Isaac Cushing
The Second Owner, 1797

*For more than a hundred and fifty years after the settlement
of the town every farm-house was a manufactory, and
almost every manufactory was a farm-house. The farmer's
wife and daughters carded the wool, prepared the flax
and hemp, spun the yarn, wove the cloth, and made it
into clothing to clothe the inmates of the household.*

—*History of the Town of Hingham, Massachusetts*

When the Colonel leaves Hingham, his brother Isaac buys most of his property: the house on School Street, his share in the "old mill stream," one-third of the sawmill, twelve and a half acres of upland and meadow, thirteen acres of pastureland, half of the "long bridge" meadow, and two-thirds of a pew in the Meetinghouse of the First Parish. Isaac pays him $2,700 for all of it, expanding both his real estate holdings and his influence in town.

Isaac, the youngest of the three Cushing boys, is also an accomplished man, but his work is closer to home. In Isaac we see the strength of the family religious beliefs. A deacon of the First Parish, he is immersed in commerce and civic affairs.

Considered one of the "new leaders" in town, he is a well-known figure as he goes about his work, and no one mistakes him on his way to Sunday meeting in his fine hat, vest, and tailcoat.

—————◆◆—————

Isaac and his wife Mary are fifty-one and forty-seven when they move into the house on School Street, and several of their children are grown. Joanna is married, Isaac Jr. has left town for a job, and Sally is soon to be wed, so only the younger boys—Thomas, fifteen, Adna, twelve, and Martin, nine—are at home. They are busy; there is always something to do on a farm. Cows, oxen, sheep, chickens, and hogs have to be tended. Hay has to be put up and crops harvested. When they are old enough, they work at the sawmill. New England farms and businesses still turn on the work of families in this time before the full force of the Industrial Revolution sweeps across the land.

During the day, Isaac is at the sawmill, managing crops, or doing the church's work. He and his older brother Jacob farm adjoining lands and from Jacob's surviving account books, we know they plow with oxen, take goods to the harbor by horse and cart, and hire workers by the day. We know they grow hay, corn, and rye, and that on one day Isaac buys a "beaver hatt" and on another gunpowder. We see they are men caught in change. Raised to run self-sufficient households, they are now part of a newer commerce. While they haul agricultural products to the harbor for shipment to Boston and beyond, they still buy apples, cloth, cheese, and meat from their neighbors.

The Dirt Road

The road in front of the Cushing house is a farmer's path worn into being by horses, oxen, and wagons. Less than a half-mile long, it runs between the more heavily traveled roads of Main and Pleasant streets. In thirty years, it will be called Back Street. In eighty years, it will become School Street, but nameless dirt roads are confusing, which is why, from the beginning of this story, it is School Street.

When Isaac leaves home for the Meetinghouse, he turns north. He may go on horseback, but often he walks. He passes his neighbors' farms and then the two small schoolhouses and the cemetery. To his left is the town Common. Crossing over Main Street, he walks through the cluster of small businesses and home industries. To his right is Lewis' Inn and tavern in front of which a fledgling buttonwood tree has been planted. Then he heads down Pear Tree Hill past the oldest homes.

Everyone he meets, he knows. He knows their parents and their children and where they worship and what their politics are. If you walk that same route today, you will pass the same cemetery and the same Common. The boundaries have altered— the Common is smaller, the graveyard larger—but they retain their connection to the past. Along the way are modernized houses and, of course, cars, but many of the buildings and trees are quite old, and you can still sense the path Isaac walked. But you won't know anyone.

Isaac's church, the First Parish, stands today on a hill over-looking Main Street. It is the only seventeenth-century Puritan meetinghouse in the country still in use. Constructed with wood from local forests, it was built over three days in July 1681 by the founding fathers. They were a homogeneous group, the fathers, Puritan Protestants who left England seeking a place to practice their religion, one based on the Bible and free of Catholic beliefs. Puritan values—simplicity, piety, and hard work—are reflected in the church's architecture. The building's interior is sparse, but by the time Isaac is a deacon, the congregation has changed. It is still Protestant, but the strict beliefs of the founders have given way to a more moderate Unitarianism.

The church's name changes over the years. It is the First Parish, the Meetinghouse, the Old Church, and at some point, it is nicknamed the Old Ship. Whether in reference to the construction of the building or to the ship of God has never been sorted out, but the name sticks.

—————◆—————

Isaac and Mary bring in the new century from their new home. A revolution in the way people work and where they live is brewing, but on School Street, the church, the seasons, and the farm still dictate life. It will be Isaac and Mary's children who experience the economic and societal changes, especially their sons who eventually move to other towns and take work, not as farmers but in the trades: bookbinding, stone masonry, and bricklaying. Even the news percolating across the nation has little effect on their lives. The Louisiana Purchase, Ohio's statehood, and Lewis and Clark's journey all make for great discussions, but are far removed from daily life. On the other hand, Isaac is much concerned about British interference with American merchant ships and crews as his business and the town's maritime industries are at stake. It is infuriating to consider that it will take another war to resolve the problem.

Blessed are the Dead Who Die in the Lord

Summer's end finds Mary in her garden, tangled now as it is with herbs, pumpkins, turnips, and beans. The birds are picking off the last of the berries. The wind has an edge for all its warmth, and already the days are noticeably shorter. Deer come in for fallen apples, and on an early morning, there is a rabbit in the garden. Bluebirds are forming flocks, and at night, a fox raids the hen house. A great blue heron perches on top of the barn from time to time, and on most days, you can smell the sea.

———————•◆•———————

The Colonel dies in November of 1809, and Isaac may make the seventy-five-mile journey to see him in his final days or to bury him. If you go today to the North Cemetery in Lunenburg at the end of November, you can stand at the Colonel's gravesite and imagine that day as if Isaac were there, the maples and birches bare of leaves and the sunlight brittle or the sky low with clouds. Hannah in mourning. Isaac with his Bible in hand. The grave-diggers standing wait. I stood there on a winter day; I could imagine it.

Five years later, another cold November day, Isaac's brother Jacob dies in Hingham. It is 1814. He is seventy-two. These are depressing times. The War of 1812 is drawing to a close. The town is weary, weakened by more than two years of war with Britain. Its maritime and agricultural industries have been hard hit by shipping embargoes. Isaac is weary. He feels the loss of his brothers, the waning of his generation. He will die within the year on October 13, 1815 at age sixty-nine. It is autumn. Everything is dying.

Isaac is waked at home as is the tradition. His body is laid out in the front parlor in a coffin smelling of fresh-cut wood. Friends and family come to pay their respects. Candles burn and the last of fall's gold and auburn flowers are cut. Tansy, parsley, lavender, and sage are spread around the coffin. Prayers are offered. Bible passages are read and, when the time comes, the men carry Isaac's coffin to a horse-drawn wagon to be driven to the cemetery. A minister of the First Parish reads a graveside service.

A month later, we see Mary has a nice strong signature, which she uses to request her son Adna administer her late husband's considerable estate. They have it inventoried, and it is divided between Mary and the children. In addition to the house on School Street, Isaac has a share in the homestead on Pleasant Street, two-thirds of the sawmill, and a long list of other real estate that includes pastures, salt meadows, and woodlands. There is a horse, four cows, two beef heifers, twenty-seven sheep, a yoke of oxen, two hogs, farming tools, furniture, food stocks, and much more.

"Set off" for Mary is "the easterly half" of the paternal homestead. She also gets acres of land, "half the old barn & half the corn barn," and two-thirds of a pew in the Meetinghouse of the First Parish. It is decided that the house on School Street will be sold. No one in the family needs a farmhouse. They will take the cash to pay expenses, but that will be slow in coming for reasons to be revealed.

———◆◆———

Mary dies in December of 1821 at age seventy-one, six years after her husband. I know only that she is a Jones, the sixth of seven children, named for an older sister who died young, and that she marries at twenty, has seven children of her own and loses one as a child, her own Mary. She has grandchildren. She is buried next to her husband.

The Isaac Cushing family gravestone, an obelisk, sits close to the road in the Hingham Centre Cemetery near the corner of School and Short streets. It is a neighborhood cemetery, associated with no church, although when it first came into use late in the 1600s everyone belonged to the First Parish. Its large trees, leaning stones, and well-worn paths stand witness to its age. It is the cemetery of the ancestors.

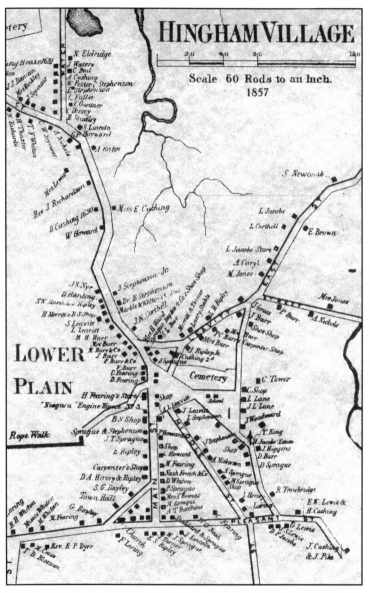

Hingham Village from the harbor in the north to the
Jacob Cushing homestead on Pleasant Street in the south.

Chapter 5

Asa Fuller
The Third Owner, 1817

*To be sold by Order of the Court at Public Vendue on Monday
the twentieth day of May next at one o clock at the dwelling
house of Isaac Cushing . . . 4 ½ acres of land with the dwelling
house, barn and other out houses standing thereon.*

—Advertisement of Isaac Cushing's Real Estate

The home of the late Deacon Isaac Cushing is advertised for sale on a Monday in May 1816, but it doesn't sell that day or on any day after that for nine months. It is unlikely the economy is to blame. The post-war years have brought business development and good agricultural prices. No, it may be something else because, even if it is sunny on the day in May the house is offered for sale, the weather is about to get uncommonly bad.

It begins when snow falls on June 7. After that, there are cold fronts and frosts every month. Peas, beans, carrots, pumpkins, and corn freeze in the ground. Then it is hot. Then it rains. Then it is dry. There is little or no harvest. Fires are lit against the cold; firewood becomes scarce. Something is wrong, and there is no answer, so people look where they have always looked for answers. They look to the skies. The total lunar eclipse on June 9, following as it did on the tail of the recent snowstorms, is suspicious. The strange red fog that dims the sun and makes sunspots visible is odd, more than odd. What is going on? Is the Arctic melting? Has the weather changed permanently? Should we move? Should we go west or south? Is God so dissatisfied with us?

No one knows and no one who is alive in 1816 will ever know the answer to what happened that year, the year crops fail and people go hungry. Around the world, it is called "the year without a summer." In New England, it is remembered as "eighteen-hundred-and-froze-to-death," but it will take scientists nearly a century to realize that before the snow falls in June, before severe food shortages in Europe lead to rioting, and before food prices skyrocket, a volcano in Indonesia spews millions of tons of gas, debris, and ash into the atmosphere, producing a dust cloud of debris that will circle the globe, obscure the sun, and affect the climate for two years. All they know in 1816 is that something is wrong. So they pray. They stretch the food they have. They feel the gloom that mingles in the air with the smoke from fireplaces that burn in summer.

Isaac's heirs wait through the summer, fall, and winter for a buyer. They are busy. They want to sell the house, so they reduce the price to $1,600, and when they finally find a buyer, they loan him the money to buy it.

Enter Asa

He comes, the buyer, in February 1817, at winter's end, out of the fog of war and bad weather. I see his name for the first time on a deed—Asa Fuller. It is disorienting, a mistake has been made somewhere, I think; the house has always been in our family.

But, no, here is Asa, no relation to us at all, right here in black and white. Who is he? What is he doing in our family story?

Asa has a story of his own, of course. Born in Westminster, Massachusetts in 1785, the year the house was built, he is the oldest of twelve children. There are portraits of his parents, Azariah and Mercy, and several of his siblings in a Fuller family history, but there is no portrait of Asa. He is a man on the move. He marries three times but never has children. He lives much of his life in western New York and southern Canada, remote sparsely populated places. Frontiers in a time when there are still frontiers.

Before the frontiers, there is the first marriage. Asa is twenty-two, Nancy Locke is twenty-one. They marry in her hometown of Waltham, Massachusetts in January 1807. They go north, and sooner than later, they are in Buffalo, New York. It is newly settled raw country. It is Iroquois country. Travel is difficult. There are no roads. The village is small. Just a few years before, a visitor reported that Buffalo is populated by "a casual collection of adventurers" with "little sense of religion." By 1810, though, the population has grown to 1,508, and there is money to be made. Asa keeps a tavern and an inn. He acquires a farm north of Buffalo near present day Niagara Falls.

Outside of that, I find no information. Why does he leave Buffalo and come to Hingham? What about all those marriages? Then I discover two of Asa's letters in a museum collection of Fuller family papers. Finally, I think, Asa will have something to say for himself. I request copies and imagine what I will learn. Of course, this is the trap the researcher sets for herself. Once received, the first letter, written by Asa on February 1, 1813, is heartbreaking and answers none of these questions.

Addressing his younger brother, "Azariah Fuller Jr., Boston, Massachusetts," Asa begins "Condesending Brother," and ends "My dear Brother I think that we shall meat again in this world if nott I hope in the world of happines." In the pages in between, he details the horrors of the War of 1812 and the battles he has witnessed. In cursive script and the spelling of the day, he writes, "battles have been Fought in my sight that would astonish you. I have seen 100 men laying & wallowing in their gore. I have seen and herd tribes of Indians yelling and fighting." He describes how the British hire "savvageies to murder americans." He laments that it has been "about six years sins I have seen Father or mother or Brothers or Sisters or any friend except those of my one makeing." He seems to chide his brother for some previous comment that the war is unpopular (the war is unpopular with many New Englanders) and advises that, "When fedrals frown and say unpopular is the war say to them that Brittish influence can nott avail for I have a brother who has seen and found out there skeams and noes them to be vilionous."

He writes about his work.

> Ower armey now lays at buffelow expecting every moment to be attacted by the Britihish and indians; bad news has just come from the wabash that Gen Winchester and his armey are taken by those hell-hounds and but for my wife I would gird on my Soard and fly to the armey and fight till victorious or dead. I am now nine miles from the armey serveing as agent for the Contractor of the armey buying and killing cattle buying flower and Whiskey. My pay is hand-som. I had allmost forgotten to tell you the Brittish and indians have robbed me of 1500 dollars worth of stock and other moveables but my life and healthe is spared . . .

In a postscript, he asks his brother to "Direct the letter that you send to Buffelow Count Niagarah State New york."

Asa has good reason to wonder if he will see his brother again, because in December, British troops and their native allies seek revenge for the burning of a Canadian village by reducing settlements on the American side of the Niagara River to ashes. "The whole Niagara frontier on the American side, from Fort Niagara to Tonewanta Creek, a distance of thirty-six miles, and far into the interior" is destroyed. Asa's house is burned. He and Nancy, if they have not already left, escape into a night that is bitterly cold. The ground is covered in deep snow and the wind is biting.

Buffalo itself will be in flames by the end of the year.

———————•♦•———————

On December 24, 1814, after three years of war, a peace treaty is signed. There is no victor. All that was gained is returned; all that was lost is restored. The British and Americans move on. The great losers are the tribes who fought on both sides. The British abandon them. The Americans negotiate treaties that strip them of their lands and result in the creation of reservations.

It is 1815. The Niagara Frontier is in ruins. Many have left, but Asa is here and he still has a farm north of Buffalo. He is also operating a tavern with his brother Azariah, who came to New York at war's end. Business is rebounding along the frontier and throughout the northeast, and the tavern is profitable for about a year. Then, it seems, Asa leaves the tavern and returns to his farm. The business fails and Azariah falls into serious debt. There is speculation in the family that Asa is in part to blame.

A year later, June 1816, Asa is in Fitchburg, Massachusetts where his parents live. He is in "great anxiety." He has a court date. His business is unclear, but it is safe to say it has to do with money or lack thereof. He plans to go back to New York after things are resolved but he does not, at least not to stay. He leaves the frontier, and eight months later he is in Hingham buying the house on School Street. I don't know why he is here.

The Third Owner

Asa, third owner of the house, supplier to the Army, tavern owner, and farmer, buys the School Street property on February 28, 1817. If any money changes hands, it is unrecorded. He takes a mortgage from the Cushings dated the same day as the deed.

It is cold when Asa and Nancy move into the house, as cold as only an unoccupied house in winter can be. There are squirrels in the attic and mice in the kitchen. Nancy goes to work with what I can only imagine is relief. How easy life is on School Street after living in a war zone in winter on the Canadian border! Asa goes to work as a victualler, a butcher.

Business is good in town, but whatever Asa envisioned when he bought the house on School Street doesn't materialize. Ten months later, he takes out a second mortgage. Clearly, he blames the war for his financial troubles, because he has petitioned the U.S. House of Representatives "praying compensation for property, destroyed by the enemy, on the Niagara frontier, in the late war with Great Britain." It is a slow process to petition the government and on Dec. 30, 1818, less than two years after buying the house on School Street, he sells it. He does not come away with much. The buyer pays him $18.64 and assumes both of his mortgages. He and Nancy move, presumably to a rented house.

A full year later, in December 1819, Asa's petition is "laid on the table," effectively denied, by the House Claims Committee. The record reads "Asa Fuller—Innkeeper; hired house etc., burnt; small family; presumed not to be in want."

In 1820, Asa is in Hingham. It is the last time I find him in a census.

At some point Asa and Nancy separate, and she returns to Waltham to live with her parents. It is not working with Asa. Maybe he is done with her. Maybe she is done following him to remote places. Maybe she has had enough of the financial ups and downs. Maybe they are out of love. Do they divorce? The 1850 federal census shows Nancy Fuller as single, living with her aging parents. Three years later, a Locke family history says she is a widow. On her death record in 1866, she is recorded as a widow. But she is not a widow. Asa is alive. He will outlive her by two years.

When he leaves Hingham, Asa looks for a new frontier. He ends up in Canada. A family historian writes that he married twice again. She found no records of these marriages, but she is writing in 1897 and Asa and his siblings are dead, so she looks to the younger generation for information. A niece or nephew remembers that Uncle Asa had three wives—"Aunt Nancy," "Aunt Patty" and another whose name no one can remember. I find Asa's last wife, Mary Jane Curtis. Although I don't find a marriage record, she is referred to as his wife in church records and is buried with him in Canada.

What does Asa do while he is in Canada? He has a farm or an inn or both. Late in life, he runs a boarding house in Sorel, a small town near the confluence of the Richelieu and St. Lawrence rivers. This is the same town where the Colonel and his men suffered from smallpox and hunger while pulling out of Canada during the Revolution, and this is where Asa dies on August 25, 1868 at the age of eighty-three. He is buried here in Christ Church Anglican cemetery.

We return now to Hingham where, on December 30, 1818, Asa Fuller sells the house on School Street. Given the number of Cushings in town, it's not so unlikely that it comes back to a Cushing descendant. That the new homeowners are Susanna and Joseph Trowbridge, my fourth great-grandparents, makes it a story.

The Trowbridges are no strangers to the house on School Street. Isaac has only been dead for three years, Mary is still alive, and Susanna knows all the Cushings in town because she is a Cushing on her father's side. Although the blood is thin, Susanna, Hannah, the Colonel, and Isaac are all related. Matthew Cushing, who arrived in town in 1638 with his wife Nazareth and five children from Hingham, England, is their common ancestor, as he is mine.

Barns and agricultural outbuildings were part of the property throughout the nineteenth century.

Chapter 6

Joseph Trowbridge
The Fourth Owner, 1819

*The avenues for transportation of people and merchandise from
Hingham to the neighboring country have been two-fold. The
boat by water and the beast by land have conveyed to the desired
destination the inhabitants and the products of their industry.*

—*History of the Town of Hingham, Massachusetts*

Joseph sees Hingham first from the sea. He is coming from Boston, sailing south past the small islands into Hingham Bay on one of the commercial packet boats that carry passengers to and from the city. Raised in a port town, he is at home on a boat, a wharf, a shore. There is something behind him and something ahead. Neither one is perfectly clear. He is twenty-eight. It is early in 1804. Why he is on the water this day is a mystery.

Joseph Trowbridge is certainly born in New Haven, Connecticut in 1776, the year the Declaration of Independence is signed. He is the sixth of nine children. Finally, they say, a son. After five daughters, a son! He is named for his father, Joseph II, who is a wealthy man, but he will not be Joseph III, merely Joseph. His mother, Sarah Sabin, is the daughter of a distiller and merchant, and the family lives in "considerable luxury" in a fine house in town. The house and the money came to Joseph II when his father, the esteemed Captain Joseph Trowbridge, died.

The Trowbridges are legendary in New Haven and beyond—the long line of seamen and merchants descended from Thomas who came to the New World from England in 1636. By the eighteenth century, they dominate the West Indies trade. Their sloops and schooners sail to the West Indies loaded with fish, beef, beans, lumber, and crates of chickens and hogs to provision plantation owners and their African slaves. They return with cargos of sugar and molasses. They profit. The town profits, and many a farmer educates his sons on the proceeds of the West Indies trade.

But Joseph II, the son of Captain Joseph, doesn't take up the family business. He is well educated, a Yale graduate, but he never works. A college publication offers, "he followed no occupation." Instead, he lives off his large inheritance and when he dies in 1793 at age fifty, the fortune is gone. "Reduced," says a Trowbridge family historian. "Squandered," writes my Aunt Ruth, who studied the family history before me.

———————◆◆———————

The father gone, things are in disarray. Joseph, seventeen, has been sent to Philadelphia to serve an apprenticeship to a watchmaker. An older sister, Eliza, has married a local man, but most of the other siblings live with their mother who, after her husband's death, turns to her sister Mary for help.

Mary lives in Colebrook, Connecticut with her husband the Rev. Dr. Jonathan Edwards Jr., a prominent theologian and minister of the church. Is this, I wonder, where the sisters' dreams of marriage die? Is it the loss of money and status or a lack of dowries that renders them spinsters? Is it the shock when they learn their sister Eliza is dead in the first year of her marriage, or is it the example of their parents' marriage? It could be any or all of these things, but it is *something*, because in a day when almost everyone marries, only three of the nine Trowbridge siblings ever marry.

At some time after his father's death, Joseph moves to Boston where he goes into business as a watchmaker or a silversmith. When he is twenty-eight, he comes to Hingham. He comes for a job, or for a change, or maybe he has a friend who knows a girl. It is time he marries. His father has been dead eleven years. His mother Sarah has just died, and all seven of his siblings, all single—Sally, thirty-seven; Polly, thirty-five; Fanny, thirty-two; Lucinda, thirty-one; Hezekiah, twenty-six; Rosewell, twenty; and Laura, seventeen—are preparing to move to Denmark, New York, a tiny hamlet not far from the Canadian border. It is a long way from New Haven, and the story of why they go to this particular place is muddled. They may have relatives there or Hezekiah or Rosewell may have found work there, but none of this brings us any closer to knowing why they leave Connecticut to live in the wilderness and why Joseph is in Hingham. But here he is.

———◼◆◼———

Susanna Burr is born in Hingham in 1786, a sixth-generation Burr in a country that is still young. Her father, Levi, makes his name on the first day of the Revolution when he marches toward the Lexington battle with a Hingham company. He is seventeen years old, a drummer.

Levi and his father are quick to arrive at the Common on the morning the alarm is raised. The militia organizes for the march to Boston, and people gather along the roads to cheer the men as they pass. According to a town historian, the weather is clear, the breeze soft and the cherry trees in blossom. The air cracks with excitement and emotions run high, but as the days wear on there is little revelry. Conditions in military camps are grim and rations lean. Levi gets sick and is sent home before his time is served. Illness is reality; dysentery, diphtheria, smallpox, and other diseases haunt the camps. Levi is lucky. Under the care of a local doctor, the bills paid by his commanding officer, he recovers enough to reenlist the next year. He is in Dorchester and Roxbury when the British evacuate Boston. A young man, he has enough stories to last a lifetime.

In the waning days of the war, Levi marries Susan Stowers—his second cousin—and they move into a new house, a Cape, at the corner of Leavitt and Short streets near the cemetery. Levi and Susan's seven daughters will be born here, and 175 years later when I walk past the house, it will bear a plaque that says "Levi Burr House, Built 1783." I will pass it three or four times a week for years on the way to the library or to school or to meet friends, oblivious to the fact my great-great-great-great grandmother, also the oldest of seven girls, was born and grew up here.

Susanna's life mirrors her mother's life. From a young age, she works beside her, making candles and soap on one day, baking bread on another. She learns how to build a fire. She can balance a baby on her hip while hanging clothes on the line. She knows how to write her name, make an apron, nurse a sick child, and help deliver a baby. She is there when her twin sisters, Hannah and Mary, are born, and she is at the cemetery two weeks later when they bury baby Mary. She is thirteen on that day and well on her way to knowing everything she needs to know to run her own household.

Susanna's world is small, measured in a mile, in a fraction of a mile. She may or may not attend school; education for girls is a haphazard affair. On Sundays, she attends services at the First Parish. She knows everyone in Hingham Centre and is related to all the old families. So it is odd that when she marries, she marries an outsider. It is not, in the family or in the town, the norm. We marry cousins or a neighbor from down the street or across the river or someone from our church. We don't marry someone from New Haven, Connecticut.

But here is Joseph.

Sunday, December 2, 1804. It is marrying time in the country. Mother Nature rests, but under wintry skies the world is stirring. In France, Napoleon has chosen this day to be crowned Emperor. In North Dakota, Lewis and Clark are building their winter fort, and a presidential election is underway. But how far away is all of this to Joseph and Susanna as they marry in the small front room of her parents' home. The fireplaces are blazing and wood smoke hangs in the air. Horses stomp in the yard. The Reverend Henry Ware of the First Parish hands his hat to one of the girls as he comes through the door. The long table in the kitchen is brimming with food. Tea is brewing. The men drink beer. The house overflows. Aunts, uncles, grandmothers, and cousins drift in and out. Children run up and down the stairs.

Life in 1804 is lived in the orbit of the family, the farm, the church, and the sea. Cottage industries and small businesses thrive. Joseph, the newcomer—he is the first Trowbridge in town—has help getting established, having married into a family of Burrs, Stowers, Cushings, and Lincolns. It is no surprise, then, that when he opens a blacksmith shop it is on land adjacent to his father-in-law Levi's property. He and Susanna live with her parents or a relative. On Leavitt Street alone there are at least seven other Burr families, all of them related to her parents, who are, we remember, second cousins.

Joseph and Susanna's first baby is a girl, Emma Cushing Trowbridge, born in 1805. A rather long six years later, their second child, Roswell, is born. It is 1811, the year of the Great Comet, that brilliant wonder, which is first seen in the spring and grows brighter and brighter, fading only in the new year. It portends war and doom, as comets do, and war does come to America the next year—a second war with Britain. It lasts more than two years and it is not until the peace treaty is written in December 1814, that Susanna and Joseph's third and last baby is born. They name her Susan for her mother and grandmother. It is warm in the room where Susanna gives birth. A crackling fire is burning, sending sparks up the chimney and taunting the cold drafts that dance through the windows and under the door. Her mother and a midwife are there. Someone is feeding the men and children. The wind howls. Off the coast, mariners report snow squalls.

A Home. A Village.

On December 30, 1818, Joseph buys the house on School Street from Asa Fuller, and the family moves in January, the coldest of the cold months. It takes days to heat the house, and even then not all the rooms are warm. The fire in the kitchen burns all day, and at night its coals are raked and covered. Before dark, other fireplaces are lit and quilts piled on beds. Emma, Roswell, and Susan, thirteen, eight, and four, fall asleep to the sound of snapping logs, popping floorboards, and drafts that swirl around the adults who move through the house, closing and opening doors. Their parents are home every night, and there is usually a single woman or two in residence, an army of unmarried females who come and go.

Joseph's business does well. Shipbuilders, millers, manufacturers, coopers, farmers, wheelwrights, and fishermen all need a blacksmith's services. He is involved in civic affairs. He votes, he runs his business. He petitions the town to widen the road that runs past his shop. He pays off the mortgages on the house. He buys some real estate; he sells timber from one of his woodlands. He moves in the world of commerce, the world of men, while Susanna's world turns inward, revolving around the house, the gardens, and the family.

Emma, Roswell, and Susan

The two tiny schools at the Centre are close to the cemetery and Joseph's blacksmith shop. Roswell attends the male school, the girls the female school. The schoolhouses are, by admission of the town, overcrowded and in poor condition. Procuring stoves to heat them is a controversial issue. Boys study many more subjects than girls who are taught the three Rs plus needlework and the Bible. In the coming years, new rules and regulations will improve conditions, but the Trowbridges will be out of school by then as there is no public high school.

Susanna sends her children out to school in the morning, and she is there when they come home. She is always in the kitchen; feeding and clothing a family is a full day's work. It would be a worry not to find your mother in the kitchen. The children are not indulged. Susanna prepares her daughters to be wives and mothers, and Joseph, raised in luxury by an indolent father, is driven to raise a son who knows how to support a family.

Roswell, the only son, is our man. He will go to work for his father in the blacksmith shop. He will marry, have children, and inherit the house on School Street. Going forward, the story is his, so we have to leave his sisters, Emma and Susan, here in this chapter. Sisters who live very different lives and die very different deaths.

———◆———

In October 1822, Emma marries at the age of seventeen. Her husband Leavitt Souther is eleven years older, a shipbuilder like his father. He is a successful man, a desirable match. They marry in the parlor on School Street. Her younger siblings, Roswell and Susan, are on their best behavior. Flowers are arranged, relatives and neighbors come, a large dinner is laid, and at the end of day, Emma and her new husband return to his family home overlooking the harbor. The house is still there, and it still has a commanding view, but it is not the same view Emma has. In Emma's day, the waterfront is alive with ships, wharves, workingmen, and warehouses. On the horizon are the harbor and its small islands, rocky bits of land dotted with sumacs and other shrubs. They are a constant, these tiny islands, a touchstone, as Emma's life rushes forward. By 1828, she has three children, and Joseph and Susanna are the grandparents of a boy and two girls.

Emma's fourth baby, Caroline, is born in June 1833. In August, Emma is dead at age twenty-eight. No cause of death is recorded, although complications from childbirth seem likely. Not that a diagnosis is needed to evoke the anguish that rattles the Souther home, shakes the distraught husband left with four young children, and washes across the small town, settling into the house on School Street where it is felt for many years.

On August 30, 1833, the *Hingham Gazette* publishes Emma's obituary. It is a prayer, a hymn.

> In this town, on Sunday last, Mrs. Emma C. Souther,
> wife of Mr. Leavitt Souther, aged 28. 'Jesus can make

a dying bed, Feel soft as downy pillows are, While on
his breast she lean'd her head, And breath'd her life
out sweetly there.'

————————◆————————

Fall arrives early, or do they just feel the cold and rain more
this year? The days are short and the nights pitch black. Then,
in November comes an extraordinary event that etches the year
1833 in everyone's memory. It is the night the stars fall. It is the
night the heavens fall in light so bright that people rush from
their beds to doors and windows to witness the miracle. Some
say the end day has come, and so it seems as meteors fall "like
snow flakes" in a "shower of fire" from the heavens, from the
constellation of Leo the lion.

It is historic, the greatest Leonid meteor storm in history,
and everyone in New England and beyond has a story about
that night. The Trowbridges have stories, but I don't know them.
Surely as long as Susanna lives, she will link the star storm to the
year her daughter Emma died, and when Roswell loses his son,
the one born in 1833, does he look back and wonder what forces
were at work the night that Leo, ruler of the heart, flung stars
from the heavens?

————————◆————————

Susan is eighteen when Emma dies, and she helps care for her sister's children—the baby is only two months old—until Everett
remarries, which he does soon. Then Susan is home on School
Street, helping care for her brother Roswell's children. The family has started to despair that she will ever marry, and when she
does she is twenty-seven, old for the day. She and her husband
Matthew Hawke Burr move into a new house on Main Street at

the top of Pear Tree Hill. She will live a long life and die of old age, but she will never have children of her own.

———————◦◦———————

During the 1830s, new businesses open. Hingham will never be a factory town—the large textile mills and shoe factories will go elsewhere in the state—but it hums with activity as small manufacturers produce boots, shoes, hats, and buckets. The shops that have sprouted like mushrooms after a rain sell gloves, dress patterns, hats, looking glasses, stationery, china, crockery, shoes, and every fabric imaginable. The newspaper prints advertisements and merchants hand out flyers and cards. There is so much to see and to buy.

The women on School Street are somewhat astonished when the heavy black cast iron stove is set down in front of the kitchen fireplace. The floorboards creak and moan, and hammers ring as the fireplace and brick oven are covered. Baffles and doors rasp as the women tussle with the new stove. It's all so new and noisy. They are not unhappy to lose the sound of the creaky wooden spinning wheel when it is relegated to the attic. Thanks to the fabric flowing out of the state's textile mills, they are no longer tethered to its wheel. Someone carries it to the attic, because more than a hundred years later, it serves as a prop in our games of witches and princesses. I never once stop to think whose hands have turned the great wheel before mine. I am young; I think I am just myself.

———————◦◦———————

When Joseph sits down to write his will in 1840, he is sixty-four. He leaves five dollars to each of his deceased daughter Emma's children and the rest of his property to his son Roswell and daughter Susan in "equal parts," subject to his "wife's right of dower." He will stop working by the end of the decade, and then he will be at home more than he ever has been. It is a busy household, people come and go all day, and sometimes he doesn't really know who is in the house. Susanna is generally there. Sometimes relatives or neighbors are in to visit. His daughter-in-law, Roswell's wife, is in the kitchen as often as not, and his three grandchildren are in and out, banging doors and dragging friends along with them. The house has always been this busy, of course. It's just that his life has slowed. Not working, he has time to think, to reminisce. How did the grandchildren get so old? Does he think about his brothers and sisters—all dead now except Laura, the youngest? How busy he was building a business and starting a family when his only brothers, Hezekiah and Rosewell, died in upstate New York at thirty-one and twenty-six. And his four spinster sisters, do they walk at night through his dreams down the stairs of the big house in New Haven, when they were young and well-heeled, when they thought a husband waited for them somewhere?

In 1850, Joseph buys a burial plot in the Hingham Centre Cemetery, and three years later, he is dead at seventy-seven: old age. The family is relieved he no longer suffers, because they watched him die. It is 1853; everyone who is fortunate dies at home.

Roswell orders a coffin from a local carpenter. The women make a shroud, and a wake is held in the front parlor where friends, relatives, and neighbors come to pay their respects. Someone that day must have noted Joseph's historic lifespan. Born in 1776 into revolutionary America, he experienced the birth of the nation and the election of fourteen presidents. I like to think that when they bury him at the end of November when snow is in the air if not on the ground, that it is remembered as a good life.

———◆——

It is a short walk from the cemetery to the house on School Street, and Susanna may take it slowly. A new life without Joseph awaits her. They have been married forty-nine years almost to the day. She looks back at the early years through the long lens of time. Her own mother was alive then and her daughter Emma, in that time before the other children, who expanded her heart in unimaginable ways, and before the long life and its loves and losses.

The heart of Hingham Centre;
the public library is on the right.

Chapter 7

Roswell Trowbridge
The Fifth Owner, 1853

FLOUR AND GRAIN
Extra family & Common Brands of FLOUR.
Also CORN, RYE, OATS and FEED.

Competition a Folly!
Our Prices Prove it!
Our Customers Know it!

Trowbridge and Litchfield

—*Hingham Journal,* May 27, 1859

Roswell Trowbridge becomes the fifth owner of the house on School Street after his father Joseph dies. He is forty-two with a wife and three children, but he remembers moving into the house with his parents and sisters when he was a child. It was big enough then that there was usually a single aunt or cousin in residence, and it is big enough now for his wife, children, and parents, but when his father dies in 1853, he has been for so many years a son in the house that it seems odd to be home without him.

Roswell is elusive. He comes together piece by piece. There is a marriage record; there are census records. He is a volunteer fireman assigned to Engine No. 1. He is a juror and a parade marshal. There are birth records for his children and grandchildren. There is a newspaper advertisement. There is a mortgage taken. And finally, there are enough pieces to put the border on the puzzle that is Roswell.

———◆———

We look back to 1832 when Roswell marries Sarahlane Jones. He is twenty-one, a blacksmith in his father Joseph's shop. She is twenty-four, waiting to get married and start her real life. It is early in September; the almanac reports low tides and cool temperatures. It reminds farmers that it is the month of Libra, time to tend to Indian corn, get "cider-presses in order," and dig potatoes. All around Roswell this work is being done, but for now, everything is light. He is young, he is in love, his father Joseph is alive, his sister Emma is alive, and the stars are in their rightful place in the heavens.

When Sarahlane moves into her husband's house, she must find it quiet and his family small; only his parents and seventeen-year-old sister Susan are at home. And it is quiet compared with the raucous household in which she grew, the seventh of eleven children, in the tight-knit enclave of family farms on the east side of the Weir River, "over the river" as the old timers say, where most everyone is related. Her own parents, Benjamin and Lucy, are both Joneses, distant cousins, descended from Robert, the early settler, who was farming the same land in the 1640s. But Sarahlane's history is deeper. It flows, like the river across their land, through her grandmothers and grandfathers, the Herseys, Burrs, Spragues, Wilders, Beals, Stodders, and Marshes who connect her to just about everyone in town. And it is the Bradfords, Peabodys, Lanes, and Aldens who take her back to the Pilgrims. So, it is more than serendipity that brings her to the house where her grandaunt Mary Jones, wife of Deacon Isaac Cushing, once lived.

———————◆◆———————

Roswell and Sarahlane's first child, a dark-haired boy, is born ten months after the wedding in the house on School Street. It is 1833, the year the stars fall. It is July, the month of Leo, a hot clean month. Winter's grime has been washed away; bedding and winter coats are flapping on the clothesline, and the sun is doing its work, healing many things.

They name the baby Roswell Junior and call him R.J. There has not been a newborn in the house for more than forty years, not since Hannah Cushing delivered her last child in 1792, and suddenly, Roswell thinks, the house is full of women. His wife's mother and sisters come, bearing pies and advice. His mother's sisters and cousins come. Neighbor women stop by to cluck and smile at his son. He and his father Joseph stay out of the way. It is a house of women. If one sees such things, it is an omen, like the stars that fall, this house full of women.

———————◆◆———————

Before R.J. is a year old, Roswell buys the blacksmith shop from his father for $800. (Joseph will continue to work as a silversmith.) Roswell wants his own business, because here is his second child Sarah, a spring baby, named for her mother. She will never be Sally or Sissie, but always Sarah, and a long six years later in 1842, comes the last baby. He is Henry for an unknown reason. It is a small family, three children.

It feels right to Roswell that his children grow up in a

three-generation household. He will probably look back on these decades, the 1830s and 1840s, with nostalgia. His father is still alive. It is a time of familiarity and constancy that will not come again, because while his children come up in the same small-town way he and his wife did, the nation is transforming. Wagon trains are crossing the Continental Divide headed into Oregon country. Impoverished Irish immigrants are pouring into the state, looking for work, and the sound of railroad construction echoes across the hills. It is exciting and uncertain at the same time, because while we are walking the same roads, conducting our traditional businesses, and attending the Old Church, industrialization and immigration are accelerating the rate of change. In the decades ahead, everyone will become a student of change, no one more so than Roswell Trowbridge.

The Village Blacksmith Fades

When Roswell inherits the house in 1853, he also accepts responsibility for his mother Susanna, but how he will support the family is the question running through his mind. The blacksmith business is gone. It provided a good income for decades, but now many of the tools a blacksmith makes are sold in stores. He is unsure what to do next. At home at night, he may pull a chair up to the fire and pick up the farmer's almanac. Spring is around the corner. His father wasn't much of a farmer, but no one grows up in the town without knowing a thing or two about hay and corn and livestock. The land is his now. What will he do with it?

First, he needs a job. Businesses are hiring. In this town alone there are coal dealers, grocers, carriage makers, carpenters, painters, box makers, and other manufacturers. He chooses shoemaking—it's a going concern. The town employs many workers and produces thousands of pairs of shoes and boots a year. This will change as mechanization streamlines the industry and the big factories go elsewhere, but for now business is good.

R.J., Sarah, and Henry

When their grandfather Joseph dies, R.J. is twenty, Sarah seventeen, and Henry eleven. R.J. is a shoemaker, Sarah is at home with her mother, and Henry is in school. Soon, Sarah will fall in love with Joe Litchfield, who is also a shoemaker, marry him, and he will move into the house. Henry will grow up and go to war. Before then, death will diminish the household.

After Sarah marries, there are three shoemakers living on School Street—her father, brother, and husband. They work six days a week, twelve hours a day. It is tedious work done in notoriously small overcrowded workshops. One day, R.J. gets sick; his cough hangs on. A doctor is called to the house. Consumption, he says. Tuberculosis, we will say. His mother, grandmother, and sister care for him at home. They use the best of remedies— elixirs, rest, and fresh air—none of which have any effect on his bloody cough or debilitating pain. Antibiotics will not be available for eighty years, and germ theory is not well understood. Consumption, however, is well understood. It kills you.

R.J. dies in January 1858 in the house on School Street where he was born in 1833, the year the stars fell. He is twenty-four years, six months, and seventeen days old. It is a bad start to a bad year. An ill wind blows relentlessly across the state, and R.J. becomes a statistic: In 1858, more people in the state die of consumption than any other disease. He also becomes a medical opinion: Shoemakers in their small workshops are harder hit by consumption than farmers in their fields.

There is a photo of R.J. taken when he is twenty-one. It is tiny, about two inches square, deteriorating—miraculous, I think, that it isn't gone altogether—and we see he is handsome with his dark hair, short beard, and striking features. His lips are full, his nose straight and strong, and his eyes large and dark.

They wake their boy at home and bury him next to his grandfather Joseph in the Hingham Centre Cemetery. His gravesite is marked with a small stone engraved "R. T. JR." Standing over it, today, I wonder, when they buried him on that cold January day, was there a pale young woman among the mourners who hugged her coat tight—a girl for whom he had hung the moon?

⸻ ◆ ⸻

Roswell leaves shoemaking after his son dies. It's an easy decision. The Panic of 1857 triggered a deep depression that shattered the business along with many others. His next decision is more problematic. He applies to the town for a liquor license, a controversial decision if there is one. Alcohol consumption has become taboo. Abstinence societies are active in town, and preachers decry its use from the pulpit. Politically, the sale of liquor is a hot potato. From year to year, town leaders vacillate on whether or not to allow it. This year they grant Roswell a license, but it is the only one they issue.

Why liquor? Opportunities are scarce in a depression, and Roswell must want to run his own business again. So while he is working out what to do next, he sells a good deal of rum, brandy, gin, and whiskey. The controversy probably doesn't bother him. He has many friends, relatives, and allies in town, and his plans for the future are more conventional. He plants Indian corn and joins the new Agricultural Society. He talks to his friends, he makes some deals, and in 1859, he opens a flour and grain store on Main Street in the Centre. It is a family business. His daughter Sarah's husband Joe leaves shoemaking to become a partner, and his son Henry goes to work as the store clerk.

Roswell becomes an advertiser, promoting his products and promising to earn his customers' business by offering good products at good prices. He continues to sell liquor for another year, and then he drops the license. But here he is, Roswell Trowbridge, the marketer, the entrepreneur we will come to know.

————◆◆————

By 1859, Roswell's mother Susanna is failing and with her the family's most direct link to the past; she is the only one in the house who remembers the Colonel. Her memory is vague, more legend than substance, but she talks about the old days when the Colonel and Isaac and their families were alive and when her parents were alive. Her own end is near, and she stays closer to home, although her world has always been measured in fractions of a mile. It is unlikely she is well enough to attend the first Agricultural Fair at the end of September, because a month later she is dead at seventy-three of old age. She leaves no will, but the inventory of her estate shows she has some money in the bank, a bit of land, and $62.00 "cash on hand." Her "wearing apparel" is worth $25 and her furniture $8. All of that is gone now, but the embroidery sampler she made when she was a girl remains. It may already be stored in the attic when she dies because this is where my uncle finds it 130 years later. Under the carefully rendered alphabet are the words "Susanna Burr her sampler wrought in the 14th year of her age." The stitches are faded into the cloth, barely discernible, just enough to evoke the young girl who labored over her stitches in the year 1800.

Susanna is buried with her husband Joseph and her grandson R.J. in the cemetery at the Centre—within yards of the house where she was born and a half-mile of the house on School

Street. By now, all of the leaves are on the ground and war clouds
are stacking up over the nation. There is no time to pause and
reflect on what the 1850s dealt. Everything is in forward motion.

A House Divided Cannot Stand

Roswell Trowbridge and Joe Litchfield's flour and grain store is
a busy place in the summer of 1860. Women come in to shop and
stay to talk about their families, the weather, and church affairs.
Men stop on their way from the train station and the harbor to
share the latest news from Boston. In the evening, they gather
around the wood stove, debating the upcoming election, slavery,
and the threat of civil war.

Come November, the majority of the townsmen vote for
Abraham Lincoln, and the dialogue changes. War, it seems, is
imminent, and just weeks after Lincoln is inaugurated it begins.
It will last four years and more than 600,000 men will lose their
lives. Every household has a story, but they are too many to tell,
so I tell you only the one that relates to the house on School
Street.

The war starts in South Carolina on April 12, 1861 when Confederate troops attack a federal fort. The President calls for 75,000
Union troops to put down the rebellion. A telegram arrives in
Hingham ordering the captain of the militia to "report in Boston with the Hingham company by first train." The first soldiers
leave for the front. Where is the front? No one knows exactly,
but it all seems possible, hopeful. The conflict, they think, will
be over quickly, but as time drags on and more men leave, doubt
enters into the rhetoric in the store at the Centre. Newspapers,
letters, and returning soldiers tell stories of loss and disease. It
will not be a short war, they say now, but they remain committed,

although the dismal news makes it more difficult for the town to produce its quota of soldiers. The problem intensifies and, in July 1862, Lincoln issues an urgent call for additional troops. Town leaders increase recruiting efforts and offer higher bounties. There are spirited rallies and patriotic speeches. Roswell at fifty-one is too old to serve, but Henry is nineteen, all ears and interest, and in August, he and his cousin Benjamin Jones and their friend George Merritt join the Navy.

If the walls in the Trowbridge house could talk, what would they say? I see Henry going out the side door—the same door the Colonel came through on his return from New York, the same door my father and uncle will walk through when they leave for the Second World War. I see Sarahlane following him into the yard; she has buried one son, she can't be happy to see this one go to war. I see her standing by the road, waving until he is out of sight. I see the new recruits leaving by boat; it is only a dozen miles or so by sea to the Navy Yard in Boston. They take a backward glance, but soon they are looking to the city and the South. And we look too, leaving Hingham to follow Henry, because he was born in the house on School Street, and because he has a second act in this story.

Where the Wild Wind Swept Them

The three young men are sized up, issued uniforms, and written into the record: Henry Trowbridge, twenty-one, blue eyes, light hair, 5 ft. 8 ½ in.; Benjamin Jones, twenty-nine, hazel eyes, dark hair, 5 ft. 3 ½ in.; and, George Merritt, twenty-one, blue eyes, brown hair, 5 ft. 9 ½ in. Henry and George are actually twenty and nineteen, but who is to know that.

They go south aboard the USS *Hetzel*, a "sidewheel steamer" assigned to maintain the blockade on southern ports. Ranked as landsmen, they earn $13 a month. In southern waters, they transfer to the gunboat USS *Louisiana*, "five guns," whose charter is to intercept blockade runners and support land forces. It is muggy. The quarters are close. Fear tastes like gunpowder. They have never been this far from home. George gets sick and is moved to a hospital onshore in North Carolina. He dies there in February of "swamp fever" and is buried "from the hospital." A telegraph operator sends the news north. A telegram breaks a family's heart. Later, they will place a memorial stone in the local cemetery. A publication honoring the town's Civil War dead offers these lines in his remembrance:

> Is his sleep less sweet in the land where the wild
> winds swept him,
> Than if soothed to rest at home, and kin and friends
> had wept him?

Henry and Benjamin remain at sea through the sultry spring and summer of 1863 until their time is served. They arrive home late in August by train or boat. Any celebration is subdued, because they have left George behind and because Henry is sick. The *Hingham Journal* reports this fact on September 4.

> Henry Trowbridge has been confined to his father's residence with fever, is getting better. Benjamin Jones has enjoyed good health since his return from the U.S. gunboat Louisiana, which were blockading Washington, N.C. The young and noble Merritt was one of the three from here in their company; his bones now rest on Southern soil, but his soul is in heaven.

The war drags on for two more years until, on April 9, 1865, Confederate General Robert E. Lee surrenders his army to Union General Ulysses S. Grant. Five days later, President Lincoln is shot. He dies the next morning. He will never know that the Union he upheld will persevere.

Peace

In 1865 Hingham Centre is a small village, ancient they like to say, and the old Cushing house exists in a landscape that has changed little in the eighty years since it was built. The Colonel and Hannah, Isaac and Mary, Asa and Nancy, and Joseph and Susanna are gone, but the homestead remains. Gnarled fruit trees produce crops, old wagon ruts refuse to yield, and migratory birds follow ancient instincts to nest anew in the old trees along the river.

Roswell and Joe are still doing a good business in flour and grain, but with Henry home from the war and the Northern economy booming, Roswell decides to expand the business. While life is still local, more people work outside the home and many no longer have the time or the land to produce their own food. Roswell has both; he decides to open a meat market. To finance the new venture, he takes out a mortgage on the house and buys a building that has been "improved as a slaughterhouse." A mover hauls it to School Street and sets it down on the north side of the property. Roswell puts Joe and Henry to work buying and raising livestock, and they become butchers. By the end of the decade, the store sells beef, mutton, pork, and sausages. It is a profitable business; Roswell pays off the mortgage he took on the house within four years.

A Daughter, a Son. A Widow, a Widower

In 1868 Roswell and Sarahlane are fifty-seven and sixty, parents to adult children. Sarah and her husband Joe have lived with them since they married, and Henry, recovered from the fevers that overtook him in the south, has married Mary Ordway, a farmer's daughter from Newburyport north of Boston. They live nearby in a rented house while Henry plans the house he will build. A block away from his parents' house on School Street, it will be a sizable house with enough room for a family, but Henry and Mary will never have children. No one knows that yet— that the first loss will lead to other losses or that she will never get pregnant, because every woman who marries in 1868 has a baby if she can.

Sarah's and Henry's marriages unfold, sailing through the years on remnant newlywed dreams. Sarah has two sons. Henry devotes himself to work, family, and the Grand Army of the Republic post that he and other Civil War veterans started after the war. It seems that things will go on in a similar way forever. Then as if a celestial mirror shatters, seven years of bad luck rain down. Things get out of order. Stories get cut short, and in the absence of memoir, dates and death records become the story.

It begins at the end of a decade when, on the day after Christmas 1877, Sarah's husband Joe dies. He is forty-six, dead of lung congestion. Then on February 1, 1883, Henry's wife Mary dies at thirty-eight of "septicemia," a massive bacterial infection, the cause of which is unrecorded. They bury Joe in the family plot in the Centre, but, although they have been married fourteen years, Henry does not bury Mary in Hingham. Instead he takes her body to her hometown of Newburyport for burial and comes home alone at winter's end to bare-boned trees and a slate gray sea.

Roswell and Sarahlane learn that the worry of parenting is never really over. Sarah and Henry are widowed, and their grandsons have lost their father. Sarah may wonder in her grief if her life will ever change or if fate has already written her story. Henry has no such thoughts.

The Irish Woman

It is 1884. Henry's year of mourning is over, and he is looking for a wife. His search will take him out of town, and his choice of brides will brew a Celtic wind that will rise and slowly gather force, eventually sweeping down School Street, rattling more than the windows in the old Puritan homes. Because, this is it, Henry, forty-one years old, descended from the English Protestant founding families and himself a member of the First Parish, the Old Ship, where he holds a pew, will marry a twenty-five-year-old immigrant Irish servant, and he will marry her in the Catholic Church. He will bring her home, settle her into the house on the corner of Pleasant and Union streets where he lived with Mary, and soon, she will be pregnant.

———◆———

Hannah Ferris has been in the States for about four years when she marries Henry. She is a domestic servant in Worcester, an industrial town about sixty miles west of Hingham. She is one of the many young women who left rural Ireland seeking a better life and who now work as nannies, laundresses, cooks, and maids for well-to-do families. They feel the slap of prejudice, but they view their situations as temporary. They are young and social; they have come to the land of opportunity. They send money home to their families in Ireland, paving the way for siblings to join them. Eventually, they will leave service to take jobs in factories, move in with family members, or marry. Those who marry meet their husbands at church or through a friend in the Irish community. But how do Henry and Hannah meet? It is unlikely he is in Worcester, so someone who knows Henry knows Hannah or vice versa. In the early 1880s, there are dozens of Irish families in Hingham. Many of them, farmers, teamsters, masons, laborers, have been here since the famine years of the 1840s. Prosperous families employ live-in Irish servants some of them recently arrived in the country. Did one of them introduce Henry and Hannah? I don't find a connection, but there is one.

The Reverend Thomas Griffin marries the couple in the Catholic Church in Worcester on the first of July. Hannah's older brother James would have been there that day—he must be in town because he will marry here in six months—but I'm not so sure there is anyone from Hingham in the Catholic Church that day.

Hay is being made, the potato bugs are out, and forget-me-nots are blooming when the newlyweds return to Hingham. We wonder what kind of welcome Hannah gets from the School Street household. Henry's sister Sarah is supportive, I imagine, unless we disbelieve my grandmother and great-aunt who say she was a kind and generous woman. Whether it matters to Sarahlane and Roswell that their son has married an Irish Catholic, we don't know, but the town is another matter. Juicy gossip is a hard thing not to share. The deep-rooted Protestant families would have had a thing or two to say about Hannah. Irish, Catholic, and in service! Surely there is a lot to say about that. Prejudice against the Irish runs deep. New England Yankees still dominate business and society, but what may not be clear in 1884 is that the old families are a static lot. The new immigrant population is growing and rising through the middle class, and it isn't

British. In Boston, even now, an Irishman is running for mayor, because while the Yankees hold the purse strings of finance and commerce, the sheer number of Irish immigrants will rise and have their voices heard.

Hannah's story could be a book in itself, but why do we care about her? Her husband Henry was born and grew up in the School Street house, but she never really lived there. We care for two reasons: she is the first Ferris in town, and she is a good older sister. She takes her immigrant brothers in when they come to her and lets them stay for so long that two of them marry Hingham women, and one of them becomes my great-grandfather.

Hannah was not easy to find—a woman in history is not easy to find—and it took a long time. Primarily because I wasn't looking for her. Information about my great-grandfather was vague and much of it hearsay, yet it set me on a path to what is true. On this path, I found Hannah—the sister no one really knew about or thought to mention.

The Gate of Heaven

1885. Roswell and Sarahlane are aging; they will be dead within two years. Today, we can see the world they live in, because a large illustrated bird's-eye view map of the town is printed this year. We see the Trowbridge house on School Street with its barns, fences, and outbuildings. Two men are sketched in the yard. A block away is Henry's house on its corner, a tall narrow structure with a stable in the back. Down the street, we see the Centre cemetery, its gravestones, paths, and trees carefully rendered.

July 1885. Sarahlane is dead of pneumonia on the Fourth of July; she is seventy-seven. The family gathers in the cemetery to bury her in the family plot. Relatives, neighbors, and the women of the Centre Sewing Society form tight knots around the gravesite. It is hot and muggy, but we can hold this image in our minds, because eight months later, they are back to bury Roswell. The landscape is bleaker and there are more men—business associates, the fire department, and other friends—but the place is the same. Roswell is dead of heart disease at seventy-five. Or maybe, he is dead of a broken heart. He and Sarahlane knew each other their whole lives. Science says it happens. I'd say it did.

There is a photograph of Sarahlane. In the portrait, she stares straight into the camera, but it is difficult to judge her age. Is she fifty or sixty? Her face is wrinkled, her lips a thin tight line. Her face and neck show signs of age, but her hair is raven. Her black dress is full, intricately pleated and darted and you can almost hear its stiff folds crinkle. A narrow white lace collar fastened with an oval brooch is her only embellishment. The book she holds in her right hand must be a Bible. If Roswell has a portrait taken at the same time, it is lost. Although surely a photo is taken of him at some time, and I peer expectantly into the old Agricultural Society photos, wondering which one of the gray-haired, gray-bearded men he might be.

In death, Sarahlane is recorded as the wife of Roswell. Roswell is recorded as a blacksmith. Although he was a shoemaker, a liquor salesman, a grain merchant, and a butcher, in death, he is remembered by his first occupation, the occupation of his father Joseph. Then we remember, his father was the first Trowbridge to live in the town and it is still a small town and in that small town way, you are always your father's son.

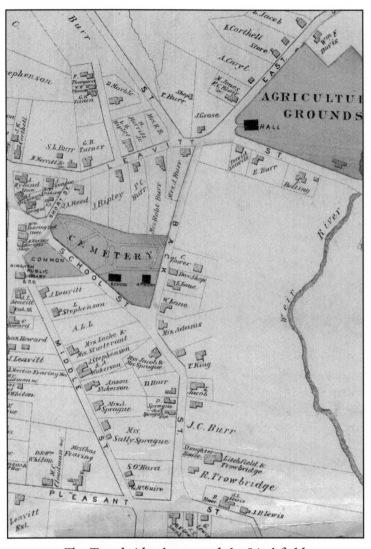

The Trowbridge home and the Litchfield
and Trowbridge slaughterhouse are near the
intersection of Back and Pleasant streets.

Chapter 8

Sarah Trowbridge Litchfield
The Sixth Owner, 1886

*She was a woman of highest integrity, calm through
trial and tribulation, of a sweet and gracious disposition,
well beloved by all who knew her and an inspiration
to those with whom she came in daily contact.*

—Sarah Litchfield Obituary

The widow Sarah Litchfield inherits the house on School Street
when her father Roswell Trowbridge dies in 1886. She is fifty, the
house is 101, and fate and circumstance have conspired to make
her the first woman to own the house. The vernal equinox is
two weeks away, but already the ancestral moon has turned the
tide—from this day on only women will own the house.

Time warps, contracts, and expands in this house so fre-
quented by the past. Sarah's husband, brother, grandparents,
and parents died here, all while she lived in the house. But
today both of her sons and a daughter-in-law live with her, and
they are looking ahead. So she looks ahead. The past isn't going
anywhere.

Seeking Sarah

Sarah Trowbridge, daughter of Roswell and Sarahlane, grand-daughter of Joseph and Susanna, is hard to envision. She is born in 1836, so this is part of it. It is a time when men live in public spaces and women live in the home. It is the men who hold jobs, vote, pay taxes, fight in wars, make laws, and write history. Our Sarah is particularly hard to see, because she lives her life in a multi-generational household; she is one of so many. The house is never really hers to run until her husband and parents are dead, and by then she is fifty years old. She is also invisible in the physical sense in that the only photo I have of her is blurry and taken at a distance. However, in this one indistinct image she is, aptly, standing in front of the house on School Street. There are photos of her brothers R.J. and Henry taken when they were twenty-one and twenty but not one of her. Was one not taken on the occasion of her twenty-first birthday or did no one save it?

I do know that the house on School Street is her most val-ued possession and she will make every effort to keep it in the bloodline—to bypass her widowed daughters-in-law and ensure it goes to her granddaughters.

And that is a story I can tell you.

———◆———

Sarah's story begins, like that of many nineteenth-century women, when she marries. She is twenty, her groom Joe Litch-field is twenty-five. It is Christmas Eve 1856. The household is bustling; her parents Roswell and Sarahlane, her grandmother Susanna, and her brothers R.J. and Henry all have work to do. The house smells of roast turkey or maybe ham and molasses. Potatoes, gravy, and cranberry sauce are being prepared. Pies are set to cool on the kitchen table. Fires are built up. Chairs are carried into the parlor. The wedding cake is on display in the dining room. Evergreen boughs have been placed in vases, but there are no Christmas decorations. The holiday is not widely celebrated, and in this household Puritan values hang on.

The house is warm and welcoming. More so because outside it is bitterly cold. Last night's snowstorm and high winds cracked tree branches and drove ships to ground along the coast. Today though, the roads are passable in some manner; the minister has arrived at least. He performs a short ceremony, dinner is served, people stay to visit, and at the end of the day, Joe moves into the house. This must be a temporary solution, I think. Sarah has two brothers at home, and she and Joe surely want a house of their own. Or so the thinking would go, but no one is thinking very far ahead, and if they are, they don't factor in depression, death, disease, and war.

———◆———

Joe Litchfield comes to Hingham from the neighboring town of Scituate flying his old name as if he has always lived here. Baptized Joseph, he is descended from Lawrence, the progenitor of the New England Litchfields, who was farming in Scituate in the 1640s. It is through Joe, my great-great-grandfather, that I am related to the Merritts and the Lincolns.

Joe is a shoemaker like Sarah's father Roswell and brother R.J.; maybe this is how she meets him. He is quickly involved in the town. He becomes a volunteer fireman and joins the Centre baseball team and the Old Colony Lodge of Freemasons. After R.J. dies, he goes into business with Sarah's father, and three years later, in June of 1859, he is himself a father.

The river behind the house is running low and the days are

long when the baby is born. Inside it is hot. The front windows are shuttered against the sun and the flies are thick, but the nights are cool. They name the new baby Roswell for his grandfather and dead uncle. Fortunately, for us, they nickname him Rozy. The third Roswell to live in the house, he will be an only child for ten years and then he will have a brother, but not until the Civil War is fought and won.

———————◼◆◼———————

When the war comes, it rattles and rallies the town. Young men enlist, and women, children, and old men take over the farm work. The news becomes all-important. Newspapers issue daily reports on local soldiers and distant battles. Sarah's brother Henry joins the Navy, he is single and sees adventure, but her husband Joe does not enlist. Then, in 1863 comes the draft. It is a hugely unpopular program, but towns have quotas to meet. The fact that wealthy men can buy their way out for $300 adds to the resentment. Three hundred dollars is a huge amount of money, half to three-quarters of a workingman's yearly earnings. There are heated debates, there are riots in the cities—it is a "rich man's war, and a poor man's fight"—but recruitment goes on.

Joe registers and reports as ordered. On August 28, 1863, the *Hingham Journal* publishes a list of twenty-nine men who have been exempted from service. Ten of them have paid the $300 commutation fee. One is the "only son of aged parents," two are "aliens," and sixteen are disabled. Reuben Sprague has lost an eye, George Hobart has epilepsy, Charles Stephenson has a "feeble constitution," and a number of men have "insufficient" teeth. Joe Litchfield has an undisclosed "disability." He is thirty-two.

Two years later, the Confederacy surrenders, ending the war. Men straggle home, losses are mourned, daily life resumes, peace settles, and in 1869 good fortune comes to School Street.

After ten years, Sarah has a second child, a second son. They name him Wilbur. Sarah and Joe will never leave the house now.

———————◆◆———————

U.S. Census Marshal Hawkes Fearing arrives at the house on School Street on Tuesday, June 21, 1870. Someone answers his knock, one of the women probably. They know Mr. Fearing and his family, and he is careful to record the three-generation household. Here are Roswell and Sarahlane Trowbridge, fifty-nine and sixty-two; Joe and Sarah Litchfield, thirty-six and thirty-one; and their sons Rozy, ten, and Wilbur, seven months. He also notes a thirteen-year-old domestic servant, Addie Hersey, in the house.

When the 1870 census is tallied, it reports 4,422 residents in Hingham, only seventy-one more than a decade before. The war years were hard, but the economy is booming, at least in the North, and the town is growing in breathtaking ways. There is new construction. There is a public library in the Centre, and a wealthy landowner is building a grand Victorian-style amusement park on the water. The first public high school is being designed, and everywhere roads are being leveled and straightened. On a hill overlooking the Square a monument to the town's Civil War dead is dedicated with great ceremony. A page turns. They will never forget the war, but it is behind them now.

A Higher Sphere

The financial panic of 1873 stresses the town's businesses, but the meat market that Roswell, Joe, and Henry opened after the war insulates them from the downturn to some degree. They probably extend more credit and take more in trade, but these are familiar ways of doing business. Then, just as the country is crawling out of the financial trough, Joe Litchfield dies. It is the day after Christmas 1877, two days after his twenty-first wedding anniversary. He is forty-six. He has been under a doctor's care for several weeks. The diagnosis is vague: lung congestion.

Tradition is followed. Joe is waked at home and buried in the family cemetery. Tradition is a comfort of its own. We know what to do. Family and friends arrive, and a minister of the First Parish, the Old Ship, performs a service. The next week the men of the Centre fire station, Niagara Engine Co. No. 3, submit a memorial resolution to the newspaper.

> Resolved, That while we deeply regret the loss of our late associate, Joseph H. Litchfield, we also recognize God's goodness in removing to a higher sphere one who was endeared to us by many ties of friendship and affection, a man of strict integrity, courteous and obliging in his intercourse with his fellow citizens, and highly esteemed by those who knew him.

Sarah, forty-one, goes into mourning. She will never remarry. She will never leave home. She will raise her sons and care for her parents until they die. She herself will die here, in the house on School Street where she was born, but not until she has buried both of her sons.

A Tale of Two Brothers

We know that Rozy and Wilbur grow up with their parents and grandparents. We see them as boys, attending school, playing baseball, building rafts to float the river, and raising animals to enter in the Agricultural Society fairs. The harvest fair is a highlight of the year; schools and businesses close so everyone can attend. The year he is nine, Rozy wins 50 cents for his prize lamb, and when Wilbur is ten, he is awarded $1 for his "fat sheep." Two years in a row, Wilbur's "black bantam chicks" win cash prizes, and the family participates in the fairs for years to come.

When his father dies, Rozy is eighteen. He works in the family business, as he knew he would. His earliest memories are of trailing after his father and grandfather while they worked in the animal pens, barns, and slaughterhouse. In the absence of his father, his grandfather Roswell becomes his mentor, teaching him accounting and marketing and working with him to adapt the butcher shop to changing customer needs. His grandfather is a marketer, and he will become a marketer. His Uncle Henry is farmer, butcher, and meat cutter, all skills Rozy learns. It is now a three-generation family business.

Wilbur, just eight years old when his father dies, is a good student. He is one of seven from Centre Grammar who will qualify for admittance to high school. He will not go into the family business, but will hone his interest in science and create a career of his own.

The brothers join the fire department when they are eighteen, albeit ten years apart. Looking at their department portraits, you would not see them as brothers. Rozy has a sparkle in his eye and a hint of a smile that shows under a heavy mustache. Wilbur is younger, clean-shaven, all seriousness and big ears, but the superintendent badge is visible on his coat and you can sense his earnestness.

Rozy will advance steadily through the ranks, becoming foreman of Hook and Ladder No. 1 Company. He will become Chief Engineer. He will be titled Captain. He will fight fires and keep the record in his hand. He will represent the town at state events and participate in parades, dinners, and meetings. And when he dies at age fifty, townspeople and businesses alike will lower their flags to half-staff, and the firehouse bell will toll his age.

Wilbur will chart his own course through the department. He will take an interest in the new technology of fire alarm systems. When he dies at age forty-one, the entire fire department will attend his service and escort his casket to the cemetery where he will be buried near his brother.

Two Brides, One Baby

Rozy and Wilbur will die young, we know this, but in the summer of 1884, when Sarah is forty-eight and her boys are twenty-five and fourteen years old, she is thinking about what to wear to Rozy's wedding. She is telling her brother Henry about the plans for the day. Henry is distracted, though, in a few weeks he will marry the Irish woman.

——◆——

Weddings

> Litchfield-Sprague—In South Hingham, 8th, inst, at the home of the bride, by Rev Alfred Cross. Roswell L Litchfield and Miss Martha Sprague, second daughter of Seth Sprague of South Hingham.
>
> —*Hingham Journal,* June 20, 1884

Sarah approves of her son's choice of brides. The Spragues are a respected old family, and she is related to them; her great-grandmother Leah was a Sprague. The wedding is lovely.

Martha is stylish, and the gardens on Main Street are resplendent. After the festivities, she and Rozy go home to School Street where she becomes a new presence in the house, a sea change. Unburdened by its past, she brings new ideas and fashion. She knows that someday the house will belong to them. We know it won't, but that June when roses are in bud and when she is so in love with Rozy, it will be.

A month later, Henry marries Hannah Ferris in a Catholic church in Worcester and brings her home to the house where he lived with his first wife Mary. Hannah is again in a foreign place, but the soft air of this seaside town is more like Ireland than that of the inland industrial town she has just left. For the first time, she has a home of her own. She is far from the small cottage where she grew up and it is impossible not to look back, not to miss her parents. She will never see them again. She will never see her sister and brothers who stayed in Ireland. It is the price of her new life.

The baby is born in September; she is named Isabel. At forty-three, Henry is a father for the first time. In Hannah's joy is the splinter of sadness. It's hard to imagine how far she feels from home—you have to erase radio, telephones, television, airplanes, cars, and email from your thinking. You have to imagine waiting for a letter that comes by boat if it comes.

The Lord Giveth and the Lord Taketh Away

In 1887 Sarah and Henry are the only two of the family left, their parents dead within a year and a half of each other and buried with their brother R.J. With no trees to break her sightline, Sarah can see Henry's house from her front yard. He and Hannah bring Isabel across the road to visit. Sarah has no grandchildren, so her niece is a joy. I imagine Isabel is blond, as her younger brother Ray will be, and that she has curls and that she is the light in her parents' lives. She is two in September. She toddles about, chasing the cat and playing in the leaves. The weather cools, she gets a cold, and in November she is dead of croup. A tiny death notice appears in the paper: "Trowbridge—in Hingham Centre, 13th inst, Isabel, daughter of Henry and Hannah Trowbridge, aged 2 years, 2 months, 2 days."

They buy a plot in the Catholic cemetery and bury their baby. The cemetery is remote in that day, a rectangle cut from the forest at the end of a dirt road, a lonely place.

Isabel is an angel. Isabel is in heaven. The mother's prayers rise, and a year later, at the end of September 1888, a son, Frances Ferris Trowbridge, is born. The next year in November a daughter, Mabel, arrives. Then the huge blow, when Mabel is a month old, fourteen-month-old Frances dies of meningitis. It is December 15, 1889. Three infants in three years, two dead. Time stops. It is cold that day and the next. There is snow on the ground. Henry breaks ice for the hens and checks on the livestock. Then it warms. The winds are from the south and mild, and by the end of the month, the ground is brown and bare and the trees bereft.

Rosary beads clink in the parlor. Family and friends come and go. Prayers move through the house until the unbearable becomes bearable and life begins again. Henry works. Hannah hangs tight to Mabel. Of her three babies, she has only Mabel. She will always hang tight to Mabel, and Mabel will never leave her mother. Mabel will never marry, she will live with her mother until she dies, and when she herself dies at sixty-one, she will be buried with her parents.

———◆———

There is photo of the house on School Street taken in 1889, the year they bury Frances. It is a desolate month, winter or fall.

The photographer stands in the road to capture the image. The house dominates the photo, but to its left we see a large barn. Three fledgling trees dot the front yard. To the right of the house, water or ice lines the wagon ruts that lead to the carriage house. The occupants—Sarah, Rozy, Martha, and Wilbur—are not in sight, but a large dog sleeps by the front door and a small black cat studies the photographer from the corner of the house.

We look inside, beyond the photographer's view. In the kitchen, there is a tap with running water and an icebox. Wallpaper has been hung and throw rugs cover the floors in the bedrooms and parlor. Identical white tieback curtains hang in every window, and on the second floor, there is a small bathroom at the top of the stairs. The house looks comfortable, but coal-burning stoves and fireplaces are still the only source of heat. Drafts seep in around the windows, and the same mournful wind haunts the chimneys on stormy nights.

And here, I see, is where things, possessions, are carried into the future. The wooden icebox will be there when my father is a boy, and he will wait for the iceman, hoping for chips of ice on a hot day. The heavy cast iron stove will be there when I am a child, although an electric range sits next to it. A sampler will languish in the attic for another hundred years. Photographs will fade and crack in the light of many suns. Crockery and tankards will collect dust in musty cupboards.

Henry, Hannah, and four of their
children are buried in St. Paul's Cemetery.
Their gravestone, right, is topped with a cross.

Chapter 9

Frances Briggs Litchfield
The Seventh Owner, 1920

. . . he was a delightful companion to wife and children,
and the tender affection in which he always
held his mother is, of itself, a beautiful
memorial of his character. His family
will have the sympathy of a large circle
of friends in their great misfortune.

—Wilbur T. Litchfield Obituary

The Gay Nineties dawn. It is late in the Victorian era, the last decade of the century. The widow Sarah Litchfield, fifty-four years old, sixth owner of the house on School Street, is at home with her sons Wilbur and Rozy and Rozy's wife Martha. The path to the seventh owner is a winding one, and succession will not go as expected. Indeed, a number of unexpected things are about to happen. Smoke from a fire will soon drift over the house, an Irishman will come to town, new homes will be built, love will bloom, weddings will be celebrated, and babies will be born.

Smoke from a Fire

The seventh homeowner is thirty years in the future, and the family stage gets crowded over this time. So as not to lose our way, we will keep returning to the old house on School Street and Sarah, daughter of Roswell and Sarahlane Trowbridge, widow of Joe Litchfield.

The fire that gives rise to so many things starts in the pre-dawn hours of May 5, 1891 in Sarah's brother Henry's house. It starts with a wisp. A whisper. A whoosh. Henry has been up late, so when he does get to sleep, he doesn't smell the smoke at first. On May 8, the *Hingham Journal* reports this and other facts.

> The most serious fire we had for a considerable time occurred last Tuesday morning at 2:30 o'clock, when, before assistance could arrive, the dwelling of Mr. Henry Trowbridge on Pleasant Street was so far the victim of the flames as to be beyond control of the fire department and together with its contents, it became a total loss.
>
> The fire is supposed to have originated from a defective flue. Shortly after midnight, Mr. Trowbridge started a fire in an air-tight stove for the purpose of heating water for sickness; this accomplished, he retired and was again awakened by being almost suffocated by smoke. The fire had made considerable headway round the chimney and was eating its way toward the roof. The removal of his wife and child was first accomplished and then the neighborhood was aroused. Box 36 Niagara engine-house was pulled, but the department was slow to respond ... Mr. and Mrs. Trowbridge lost everything but the clothes they hastily put on and a small amount of bed

clothing. The house was insured for about $3,500 and the furniture for $1,500.

In the smoke-filled moment, Henry wakes Hannah, wraps eighteen-month-old Mabel in a blanket and they flee into the night. Henry or a neighbor pulls the fire alarm; Hannah takes Mabel across the road to Sarah's house. Although it is 2:30 in the morning, the School Street household is awake. Rozy and Wilbur, both volunteer firemen, are headed for the station. But it is the middle of the night. Men must gather. Horses must be harnessed to engines. It is surreal to watch one's home go up in flames.

They see it in dawn's light, the blackened wood frame, the charred chimney. Henry checks on his family, he cares for the animals, he files a claim on his insurance. On School Street, Sarah and Martha look after Hannah and Mabel. Maybe Hannah is sick, she is seven months pregnant, or maybe Mabel is sick. Please God, not Mabel. They have already lost two babies. The men of the fire department ruminate over the report that they "were slow to respond." The fire smolders, the chimney cools, the smoke dissipates.

Seven weeks after the fire, June 22, Hannah gives birth to a baby boy, Henry Morgan. They are living on School Street or in a rented house; their new house will not be completed for nine months.

Mr. Henry Trowbridge has completed and moved into one of three houses he is building on the corner of Union and Pleasant streets. The remaining two will probably be completed before summer.

—*Hingham Journal,* March 11, 1892

Three houses? Surprising. I assume he will live in one and rent or sell the other two. He is almost fifty and has a young family. It's money in the bank, or it could be.

The house Henry moves into is on the corner of Pleasant and Union streets. Defined as a Queen Anne, it incorporates the newest features: a bathroom, modern stoves, a hot water heater.

Mabel is two and baby Henry is nine months when they move. The days are punctuated with the sound of hammers and saws and the ground littered with wood shavings and spent nails as work on the other two houses proceeds. Help is enlisted from the family. Hannah's brother, carpenter Morgan Ferris, is swinging a hammer, and Henry's nephew Wilbur is painting, because before his passion for electricity took over, he worked for a painting contractor and we know, with the wisdom of hindsight, that he will move into one of the houses.

Really, there must be something about building a house that puts the notion of settling down into the minds of men, because here is Cupid, the god of attraction and desire, hovering above the swirls of sawdust. I see him there on high, taking his measure, drawing his bow. How else to explain that, in this spring of 1892, Wilbur Litchfield and Morgan Ferris are both struck by love? How else to explain that when Wilbur marries in June and Morgan marries in July, fate is winding the clock of the future?

1892. The Summer of Love, Part One

Wilbur, twenty-two, marries twenty-year-old Frances Briggs at her family's farm in Norwell, the next town over. The gardens, fields, pastures, and orchards are cloaked in early summer greens. Blueberries intertwine with raspberry, currant, and gooseberry brambles. Pear and apple trees are in blossom, and the heady scent of lilacs is on the breeze. Sunlight reflects off the pond, and green shoots dot the fields.

Frances is one of three children. Her father William is a farmer who cuts ice from his pond in winter and stores it to sell in the summer. In the winter, he sells coal. His family goes way, way back to Walter who arrived in America as early as 1643. Down the generations the Briggses build ships at their shipyard on the North River, sell timber, and farm. Frances' mother Charlotte is a Gardner who works as a teacher and a shoemaker before she marries. She will live a long life, and we will meet her again in this story when, in her widowhood, she moves into the house on School Street.

In a photograph, taken about the time of the wedding, Frances wears a high-neck button-front dark dress. Her hair is pinned up, her bangs are curled, and her dark almond shaped eyes are clear and serious. She is pretty maybe when she smiles, but I see nothing in the photo that is familiar, no hint of the woman I will know as my great-grandmother when she is old and I am young.

Wilbur and Frances settle into one of Uncle Henry's new houses, the one at 11 Union Street, where the paint is barely dry. Frances puts on her apron, unpacks her hope chest, and sets up her kitchen. Wilbur's studies pay off—he becomes one of the first electricians in town and the first Superintendent of Fire Alarms.

Now, this should be the time to move the story forward, following the lives of Wilbur and Frances, but in order to advance it, we have to step back and look at what else is happening on School Street in the spring and summer of 1892.

1892.The Summer of Love, Part Two

When Morgan Ferris comes walking through Hingham Centre from the train station people notice. A stranger is not all that common in this part of town. Before long they are all in the know. Here is Henry Trowbridge's brother-in-law come to visit his sister Hannah. A friendly Irishman with a big laugh, Morgan soon knows everyone in the village. He is so outgoing that people respond to him and, from the scraps of surviving story, I understand it would have been hard not to like Morgan Ferris.

Morgan and his sister Hannah, two of twelve children, were born and raised in County Kerry, Ireland in a small cottage overlooking the Lakes of Killarney. It is a beautiful landscape that today evokes castles and kings, but in the nineteenth century, it required hard work to make a living off the land.

Morgan comes to America when he is in his twenties, but it's hard to say with any accuracy because throughout his life Morgan takes four or five years off his age whenever he is asked, and every time his immigration year is reported on a census, it is different. It could be, as a family story goes, that he sailed to Canada and traveled overland to Boston where he found work as a carpenter. He has other siblings in the state—of the twelve of them, nine will immigrate—but it is to Hannah in Hingham that he comes and stays. He is sociable, he is a storyteller, he becomes friends with the firemen, he meets the neighbors, and he falls in in love with a girl who lives on School Street. What are the odds of that, I wonder?

Annie Elvira Tower is an only child, a tenth-generation Tower descended from John who came to town from old Hingham in England in 1637. Her father Oliver, a constable and a fireman, is proud of this long history and is active in the family genealogical society. I wonder how he and his wife Ann react when their nineteen-year-old daughter tells them she wants to marry this older man, an Irish Catholic with little more than a hammer to recommend him. But that's idle curiosity, because on July 11, 1892, Morgan Ferris and Annie Tower marry in her parents' home on School Street. A Baptist minister performs the service, and Morgan leaves the Catholic Church. For the record,

Annie gives her age as nineteen, which she is. Morgan gives his as twenty-nine, although, according to the register that exists today in a parish house in Co. Kerry, Ireland, he is thirty-three. After the wedding, he moves in with the Towers.

We can leave 1892 now. Our couples are married. Love is wafting up and down the street mingling with clouds of sawdust and the scent of roses, which will long hang in the air, for in this razzle-dazzle summer a prophecy is written that will not be fulfilled for twenty-five years.

New Houses on School Street

Four years later. 1896. Both of our couples live on School Street: Annie and Morgan Ferris at number 45 and Wilbur and Frances Litchfield at number 68. Annie and Morgan have a son, Oliver, born in 1894, and Frances and Wilbur have two daughters, Ruth and Amy, born in 1893 and 1895. The Litchfield house is on Wilbur's mother Sarah's property. She has given him a small lot, 8,972 square feet of her four and a half acres, for "one dollar and other valuable considerations," and for the first time since Colonel Cushing built the house in 1785, the land is subdivided. The newspaper publishes the following article on March 20, 1896.

> Mr. Wilbur T. Litchfield is to remodel one of the buildings on the Trowbridge estate into a house and will move it to the front of School Street on the northeast corner of the lot.

Notably, the reporter refers to the property as the "Trowbridge estate." Wilbur's grandfather Roswell Trowbridge has been dead for ten years, and his mother Sarah who owns the house is a Litchfield, but in this, the ancient borough, a decade is nothing. It was the "Trowbridge estate" for almost seventy years, and it isn't going to change anytime soon.

As for the new house, it has a history, because the building Wilbur is remodeling is one of the old farm buildings that his grandfather Roswell put into use after the Civil War. A mover and a team of horses pull it up to the front of the property close to the road, and Wilbur hires a carpenter to convert it into a home. To pay for it, he takes a mortgage from a local bank for $1,200 that he will pay back at $12.30 a month.

The state historical commission describes the house as a one-family residence, formerly an agricultural "outbuilding." The town calls it a traditional, but in 1896, it is undeniably modern. It has electricity, a bathroom, and a modern kitchen stove. Radiators attest to state-of-the-art central steam heat. Wilbur also installs a fire alarm "striker" and wires it to the station, but modern is relative in 1896—when the alarm goes off at night, Wilbur has to light a lantern, go to the barn, and saddle his horse.

And now that the house is finished, here are Wilbur and Frances' daughters, Ruth and Amy, sitting with their Uncle Rozy's dog Prince on the grass between their parents' and grandmother's houses. The girls, about three and five, hold their dolls. Could they be any cuter? Amy's blond curls peek out under her hat and she has a happy smile for the photographer. Ruth's long blond hair is tied on the side with a white ribbon, but she takes a more skeptical view of whoever is behind the camera. Their dolls look like them, Amy's wears a similar hat and Ruth's has the same mass of long blond hair. The girls love Prince. They sit close to him. Ruth's leg rests on his, which are crossed in a noble pose. So many things are right in the world on this day.

But hindsight is painful, because while the leaf is on the tree, the smile on the lip, the dog at rest, the historian knows the angel of death is nigh.

1900 Dawns

In the early years of the new century, the ground shifts and pressure builds as if along a fault line between the past and the future. The country is a wonder. America is a world power, the west is settled, the immense frontier passed into history. The School Street household has also changed in a remarkable way. In residence are Sarah, sixty-three, her son Rozy, his wife Martha, and two boarders. The boarders—a hardware salesman and a farm laborer—are new. Sarah's resources must be depleted. Rozy supports the household with the income from the meat market, but that is a smaller business now. The slaughterhouse is gone, the large-scale farming is finished, and with bills, taxes, and upkeep on the aging house, Sarah, the homeowner, has to do something. Taking in boarders is really all she can do.

———◆———

In 1903, the fault line quakes, and from her home on the corner of School and Pleasant streets, Sarah watches her family scatter. Transportation and technology have opened new doors, and people can't seem to resist walking through them. Her brother Henry and his family are going to Everett, north of Boston, and her son Wilbur and his family are headed to Brookline in the shadow of the city.

Sarah must understand Henry's move is necessary. He is sixty-one, too old to keep working as a butcher and a farmer in the new commerce, and his children are still young. Mabel is fourteen and the boys, Henry Jr. and Raymond, are twelve and seven. The job Henry has taken at the Navy Yard will be less physically demanding and offers a regular paycheck, but Henry leaving Hingham! She never thought she would see the day. He is a founding member of the Grand Army of the Republic Post, and two of his children are buried here. To start again in a new place at his age must seem impossible to Sarah.

Henry and Hannah may plan to come back—they rent out at least one of their houses—but once settled, they buy a house in Everett and sell off their Hingham real estate. A year later, they are back to bury thirteen-year-old Henry Jr., who is dead of tuberculosis. Over the years, they will come to visit, but they do not stay. Instead, they make a new life in the new town, and so we have to leave them here in this chapter. Only two of their children, Mabel and Raymond, survive to adulthood, and neither of them has children, so the family line ends here. Henry lives to be eighty-seven, and when he dies the Boston paper memorializes him as one of the oldest Grand Army of the Republic veterans in the state. A funeral is held and representatives from the local GAR post, the fire department, and city government attend. After a high Mass, his body is taken to Hingham and buried in the Catholic cemetery with the children who predeceased him. Four years later, Hannah will be buried next to him. Her will is revealing. She leaves her son Raymond $1,000. She leaves the house and furnishings to her daughter Mabel, and she leaves her entire savings of $3,069.71 to the Society of St. Vincent de Paul of Boston, a charitable Catholic organization.

———◆———

It is 1903; we go back to School Street. While Henry and Hannah are packing for Everett, Wilbur, Frances, and the girls are preparing to move. As a fire alarm system specialist, Wilbur's skills are in demand, and he has a job offer from Brookline. He and Frances rent their house on School Street, number 68, and move. They will return to Hingham someday. They believe they will.

My great-aunt Ruth has a story about the move. She is about ten years old at the time, but she remembers well the day her father's involvement with the fire department gets him in trouble with her mother. Wilbur has hired a large horse-drawn wagon to transport their belongings to Brookline. The horses are, predictably, fire horses, and no sooner is the wagon loaded than the fire bell rings and the horses take off at top speed down School Street headed to the station. Wilbur soon enough recovers the wagon and its contents, but Frances had a fright as she watched her furniture jostling about in a wagon swaying down the street behind some well-trained horses.

In the House Where They Were Born, Where They Lived, and Where They Died

> A charity progressive whist was held at the residence of Mrs. Sarah Litchfield on School Street last evening. There were six tables. The ladies' prize, a china egg dish, was captured by Mrs. Seth Sprague and the gentleman's prize, a paperweight, by Joshua Morse.
>
> —*The Hingham Journal*, Dec. 29, 1899

Wilbur and Henry gone, Sarah continues her involvement in the community. She holds fundraisers, lectures, and card parties at the house. Her daughter-in-law Martha invites friends for luncheons and Benevolent Society meetings. Rozy, a popular guy, is here there and everywhere. He is in parades, he is at a fire department dinner handing out cigars, he is playing Ombre, a card game that is all the rage. He is at a meeting of the Old Colony Lodge. Here is a photo of him in a horse-drawn carriage in the Firemen's Parade. Here he is with his company in the Town

Square, and here he is standing in front of the Niagara fire station in the Centre, a Dalmatian, the coach dog, sitting between
his legs.

Rozy and Martha are a popular couple. They attend fancy
dress balls, weddings, parties, and dances. They have many
friends and in the spring of 1909, they begin planning a party for
their twenty-fifth wedding anniversary. They place a notice in
the *Hingham Journal* on May 28.

> Mr. & Mrs. Roswell Lincoln Litchfield will receive
> their friends in honor of the twenty-fifth anniversary
> of their marriage on the evening of Tuesday June
> the eighth from eight to ten o'clock at Grand Army
> Memorial hall. This invitation is general. No cards
> will be issued.

It is a splendid party. The hall is decorated with ferns, flowers,
and plants. "Upward of 600 guests" attend. There is a receiving
line. An eight-piece orchestra plays. The entire town fire department turns out. The couple receives many gifts including "silver
and glassware, painted china, gold and silver coin and 'green-
backs', bric-a-brac, also many useful and fancy articles." The men
at the Central station, "Chief Litchfield's own district, gave an
elegant easy chair."

The party is long remembered, because less than four
months later, Dr. Dorr of South Hingham is summoned to the
house. Rozy is not well. The next week he is dead at age fifty.
Heart disease. Dead in the house where he was born in June 1859,
Sarah and Joe's firstborn. Wilbur is called home. He goes to the
Town Hall to report his brother's death. He knows everyone in
the building; everyone shares in his loss.

A funeral service is held at the house. On October 8, 1909,
the *Hingham Journal* runs his obituary.

Old Chief Mourned.
Dist Engineer Litchfield Buried at Hingham.
Entire Fire Department and
Throng of Associates at Funeral

HINGHAM CENTER, In the old Colonial Litchfield home on School St. where he was born, always
lived and where he died, the funeral of District
Engineer Roswell Lincoln Litchfield was held this
afternoon at 2 o'clock. The service was conducted by
Rev Louis C. Cornish of the First Unitarian church.

The mourners included the entire Hingham fire
department (11) men. Under chief George Cushing:
Old Colony lodge, I.O.O.F., Arthur L. Linscott noble
grand; relatives, neighbors, friends and former business associates numbering more than 150; Hingham
veteran firemen's association, a delegation from the
Barnicoat firemen's association of Boston and a delegation from the Abigail Adams Rebekah lodge, I.O.O.F.
of South Weymouth, Chief of Police W. I. James, Fire
Commissioner W.E. Easterbrook of Brookline and a
delegation from the Ombre club were there.

The Odd Fellows' burial service was read at Hingham Center cemetery by Fred H. Miller, acting noble
grand, and Arthur W. Hersey, chaplain. Previous
to the funeral service the entire membership of the
Hingham fire department gathered in the assembly
hall at the central fire station and held a service "in
memoriam," conducted by Chief Cushing, who in a
eulogy said that the town has lost an upright citizen,
the department a capable and faithful officer, and he
himself and every member of the fire department, a
genuine friend.

During the hour of the funeral places of business throughout the town were closed, flags were at half staff on all the fire homes in town and on many public buildings and private residences. While the funeral cortege was passing the bell in the tower of the central fire station struck 50 blows, the dead chief's age.

———◆●———

After the funeral, Wilbur and Henry and families go home to their lives in other towns, but one can't say life goes back to normal for Sarah and her daughter-in-law Martha, because things are no longer normal. The boarders are gone, and the two women are alone. They are still in mourning when they learn that Wilbur is seriously ill. He has a brain tumor. An untreatable brain tumor. He and Frances and the girls come home from Brookline to his mother's house on School Street. There, Frances, Sarah, and Martha care for him until he dies. It is a Monday. He is forty-one. Martha reports his death to the town. Two days later, May 10, 1911 the *Boston Daily Globe* carries a funeral notice.

WILBUR T. LITCHFIELD DEAD

Funeral of Brookline Wire Employee will occur at Hingham Home Tomorrow

The funeral of Wilbur T. Litchfield of Brookline will take place at Hingham Center tomorrow afternoon at 2 p.m. at the home of his mother Mrs. Sara Litchfield where he died Monday in his 42nd year in the house in which he was born.

The *Hingham Journal* prints a lengthy obituary on May 12.

Wilbur T. Litchfield

On Monday, May 8th, at his home in Hingham, after a long and severe illness, occurred the death of Wilbur T. Litchfield.

He was born in Hingham, Nov. 14, 1869, the son of J.L. and Sarah Litchfield. He was educated in the public schools of Hingham ...

Mr. Litchfield possessed a fine sense of duty and loyalty to his employers. He was a man of rare tact and unusual genius for his work and it can be truly said of him, that he never hesitated to respond promptly and cheerfully whenever the call came, whether by day or by night, no matter what the work was. By his death the town of Brookline has lost one of its most efficient and faithful servants. While it is true that such men are seldom heralded to the world as great or remarkable, it is equally true that all who knew him have been helped by the contact and are glad today that they knew him. Among the men whom he was daily associated and by the officials of the town who knew his integrity, loyalty and ability, Mr. Litchfield was recognized and appreciated as a rare and splendid type of manhood. It is a splendid testimony to his wholesome, wholehearted disposition to be able to say that during all the years he went in and out of the Town Hall, mingling freely with the officials and men of the police and fire departments, he always had a pleasant word of greeting and maintained a cheerful and happy disposition.

The funeral of Mr. Litchfield was conducted from his late home, School Street, yesterday afternoon at 2 p.m. Out of respect to his memory, the flags on all the engine houses were displayed half staff. The entire fire department of Hingham was ordered out to attend the funeral and perform escort duty from the house to the cemetery. A delegation from the Brookline Fire Department was also present, including the captain and some of the officers of the ladder company to which Mr. Litchfield was attached. The services were conducted by Rev. Louis C. Cornish of the Old Church and were simple and impressive. The contributions of flowers were very numerous and covered the casket. Interment was in the Centre Cemetery.

The Women They Left

Five women are in mourning. Matriarch Sarah, seventy-five, has buried both her sons within a year and a half. Her daughters-in-law, Martha and Frances, have each lost a husband. Ruth and Amy, eighteen and sixteen, have lost their father. At night in the dark, they ask, what has happened? How am I here? What wakes us, has a bird built a nest in the chimney or is it just the wind? Do they study the ceilings from their beds, wondering when he was last here, under our roof? How often do they wake up in the morning to learn again that he is gone—the son, the husband, the father? If the old house can absorb grief, it does it now.

Frances is distraught. She and the girls left Brookline when Wilbur was diagnosed with the brain tumor, and although she owns the house next door at number 68, it is rented and, without an income, she can't afford to live there. She has a little money in the bank, some property, but once that is gone it is gone. So they stay on with her mother- and sister-in-law in the old house, Wilbur's childhood home. He was only forty-one. A brain tumor. It is hard to understand.

It is a time of terrible tumult. The three widows face innumerable challenges. They have never worked outside the home. They have never had to navigate the world of real estate, town politics, or finance. Not that they aren't capable, but it is a foreign world and one in which women are not yet fully welcome. To stay in their home and maintain their place in the community, they will have to work together.

The Matriarch is Dead

In 1912, the year after Wilbur's death, the town publishes a business directory. There are three banks, a carriage maker, an automobile dealer, a bicycle shop, a horseshoer, seven music teachers, an ice cream store, two photographers, and seven doctors. There are many carpenters. There are three retail shoe stores and five shoe repair shops. There are two florists, three laundries, eleven lawyers, three coal dealers, and twelve dressmakers. Among the dressmakers are sisters-in-law, Frances and Martha Litchfield, who are doing business out of the house on School Street. Dressmaking is not a lucrative profession, but it is something a widow can do.

In this same year, Sarah, bowed by the deaths of her sons, writes her last will and testament. While she will have the "old silver," some furniture, and a little cash when she dies, it is the house that concerns her. It is the repository of the family wealth, left to her by her father Roswell. It allowed her to shepherd her sons into the world, now it will help support their widows. She spells it out.

> . . . to Martha S. Litchfield, widow of my deceased son Roswell L. Litchfield, the use and improvement of the northwest front room and chamber in the second story and the north dining room downstairs and the use of the kitchen halls and stairs in my homestead at the corner of School and Pleasant Streets . . . so long as she shall live and remain the widow of my said deceased son, Roswell.
>
> . . . to Sarah F. (Frances) Litchfield, widow of my deceased son Wilbur T. Litchfield, the use and improvement of all of my said homestead, not devised and bequeathed to Martha S. Litchfield as above set forth, so long as she shall live and remain the widow of my said deceased son, Wilbur.

After the life estates, she leaves her property to her "heirs at law," her granddaughters.

—◆—

Four years later, in December of 1916, a foot of snow on the ground, the widow Sarah Trowbridge Litchfield dies in the home where she was born, where she was married, and where her husband and sons died. She is eighty, and even at this great age, she is remembered as her parents' daughter.

Her obituary appears on page four where the death notices are surrounded by illustrations of Santa Claus and Christmas bells and advertisements for dolls, toys, books, handkerchiefs, and cigars. The holiday is at hand. It will be a white Christmas.

Death of Mrs. Litchfield

Sarah T. Litchfield, daughter of the late Roswell and the late Sarah Jones Trowbridge, passed away after a short illness at her ancestral home, Hingham Centre, December 18, aged eighty years.

Widowed early in life she reared her two sons, the late Roswell L. Litchfield, Dist. Chief of the Hingham Fire Dept. and the late Wilbur T. Litchfield, Asst. Supt. of Fire Alarm and Police Alarm Wires of Brookline, in the environment of the best home influence. She was a woman of highest integrity, calm through trial and tribulation, of a sweet and gracious disposition, well beloved by all who knew her and an inspiration to those with whom she came in daily contact.

Having spent nearly her whole life in the same community, she left a large circle of friends and relatives who mourn her loss. Her funeral occurred Tuesday from her late home, Rev. Mr. Schumacher of the Old Meeting House officiating.

—*Hingham Journal,* Dec. 22, 1916

———◆———

Sarah is buried with her sons, husband, parents, and grandparents. The household is in a state of upheaval. The matriarch is dead. There is a vacuum, an uneasiness, and a concern for the house and its upkeep. Frances and Martha are living on what savings they have, their earnings from dressmaking, bits of land they inherited, and the rent from Frances' house next door. But in times of upheaval comes change. Martha will kindle a new relationship with an old friend and remarry. The girls, Ruth and Amy, will finish school and look to their own lives. Frances, however, will never leave the house. She will live to be eighty-nine and, for years, the financial burden will fall on her shoulders.

Rozy Litchfield, right, in engineers' carriage
during Firemen's Parade. October 1897.

Chapter 10

Amy Litchfield Ferris and Ruth Briggs Marsh
The Eighth Owners, 1971

AMY TROWBRIDGE LITCHFIELD
School Street Hingham, Mass.

Amy's Oliver, unknown to us,
The reason for all of Amy's fuss,
Is greater to her, in every way,
Than Oliver Cromwell in his day.
A True Lover.

—1916 Skidmore School of Arts Yearbook

The widow Frances Litchfield becomes the seventh owner of the house on School Street in 1920, but not in any usual way. She does not inherit it or buy it. Instead, she parlays the life tenancy her mother-in-law Sarah left her into forty-five years of home ownership. The decisions she makes ensure things go as intended—that the house will go to her daughters Ruth and Amy.

In 1920, the house looks much the same as it has—there are new windows, doors, shutters, and paint—but the landscape is different. Flowerbeds have been created in the side yard. In the back, beyond the vegetable gardens and fruit trees, shrubs and brambles have formed thickets. Birds nest closer to the house now. It is a slow process, but it has begun. One day, you will have to imagine what it was like when the house was surrounded by fields, when the front yard was all but bare of trees, when there were horses in the barn, sheep and pigs in the pens, and hens in the yard.

A Tale of Two Sisters

Frances is in her early twenties when her daughters Ruth and Amy are born in a rented house on Union Street. In 1896, when Amy is a year old, they move two blocks to School Street. The family circle is tight; Frances' in-laws, Sarah, Rozy, and Martha, live next door. Her daughters report that their childhoods are happy. They learn to knit and sew and make jam. They walk to school and take flowers to the cemetery with their grandmother. They climb trees, rake leaves, play with the kids on the street, and fish at Triphammer Pond. In the winter, they ice skate and go sledding. On Sundays, they attend services at the First Parish, the Old Ship, and sometimes, if their pleas are answered, they are allowed to go to the firehouse to play with the coach dog. All of the firemen know them as Wilbur's daughters and Rozy's nieces, because Wilbur and Rozy are still alive in these childhood years.

The village of Hingham Centre is tight-knit socially and geographically. At the north end of School Street are the Common, the fire station, the cemetery, the new two-story school, and the small shops. Across from the Common is the library. At the south end of the street are the two Litchfield homes, Wilbur's and Sarah's. Along the way, are a dozen or so houses, including one owned by Morgan and Annie Ferris.

The Ferris Children

We have to go back to 1892 and the summer of love to remember Morgan Ferris, who comes to his sister Hannah's house and stays until he marries Annie Tower. They buy a house on School Street and have three children. Morgan is an excellent carpenter and easily finds work; over the years, he builds many houses in Hingham and Cohasset.

The Ferrises are key to our story because their first son, Oliver, a cute boy with an arresting thatch of dark hair and blue eyes, will become my grandfather. He has a sister Kathyrn and brother Gordon, who we can't follow without straying too far from the story, but it is important to say that all three of them live their entire lives on School Street. Oliver will marry and move to number 74, and Kathryn will marry and move to number 41. Gordon will live with his parents at number 45 for most of his life. He will marry, have one child, and divorce. Gordon is, they say, the black sheep, and after his mother Annie is dead, he will wander about until he dies in Boston, this black sheep, on the street, of pneumonia and exposure. "Old Joe Barleycorn finally got him," says my uncle. And they will bring him home and bury him in the cemetery at the Centre.

All three Ferris children go to the Centre Grammar School, a six-room schoolhouse where their children will go and where I will go. They graduate from the public high school. During the summers, Oliver works for his father shingling roofs and framing houses. Someone has higher expectations for him, however, because when he graduates from Hingham High, he enters

Harvard Dental School. Why he drops out after a year, comes home, and goes to work for his father, is history lost.

The Litchfield Girls

While the Ferris children are growing up at number 45, the Litchfield girls, Ruth and Amy, are growing up at number 68. When they are about ten and eight years old, the family moves to Brookline for their father's job. Eight years later in 1911, he is terminally ill and they return to Hingham and their grandmother's house. After he dies, they stay on. In the fall, Amy enrolls in Hingham High, and Ruth goes to the New England Baptist School of Nursing in Boston. When Amy graduates, she begins a two-year program in Domestic Science at Skidmore School of Arts. Frances, the mother, is determined that her girls will be educated, that they will have something to fall back on should they need it.

Skidmore is in Saratoga Springs, New York, a great distance away. A Christian school, it aspires to prepare young women to earn their own living through dressmaking, millinery, food preparation, typewriting, bookkeeping, and teaching music and domestic arts. Advanced for the day, women's work is still defined by the time. School rules are strict. Parents are assured their daughters are closely supervised; female faculty members live in the dormitories. "Gentlemen callers" are seen in the reception room, and all Skidmore "girls" are required to dress formally for dinner and to wear hats and gloves if they walk to town. White dresses are required for weekly meetings of the Christian association. Amy's trunk is shipped. It is too much to wrestle from trolley car to train, and it is a long trip from Hingham to Saratoga Springs. Cars are appearing on roads, but horses still outnumber them, and there is no car at the house on School Street.

———————◆•—————————

In the summer of 1915, Amy finishes her first year at Skidmore, and she and Ruth are home for the summer. The town's population has grown to 5,264 and settled into residential respectability. Gone are the manufacturers and commercial ventures of the nineteenth century. Progressive-era ideas are being applied in town. The Village Improvement Society is promoting paved roads, new playgrounds, and adequate streetlights. The beach is being cleaned up, the Town Brook is being cleaned up, and there are new trashcans along the streets.

The sisters remember summers nostalgically. They take the streetcar to fairs and plays. They walk to the top of Turkey Hill where, on a clear day, you can see the Boston skyline and to the ocean at Nantasket, following the railroad tracks. On hot, muggy days, they meet their friends at the bathing beach at the harbor. They go to dances and dance with local boys. They follow baseball; their father loved baseball. It is a bright and beautiful summer. It is the summer Amy Litchfield falls in love with Oliver Ferris, or the summer he falls in love with her, because who is to say exactly when this happened. They have lived on the same street since they were babies.

Fated Love

You might, if you looked at the 1892 registry of marriages, wonder if fate played a role in the union of my grandmother Amy and grandfather Oliver, because there in old-fashioned cursive on the same page are recorded the marriages of their parents Wilbur and Frances Litchfield and Morgan and Annie Ferris. Or you might wonder if you were alive then, if it was written in the stars, which were so brilliant before electric light dimmed them. Or if you knew the family history as far back as 1884, you might say that it was destiny set in motion the day Henry Trowbridge brought his second wife Hannah Ferris to town.

You might say all that and more, because twenty-five years after that razzle-dazzle summer of 1892 when sawdust and love hung in the air and two couples married, their children marry.

———————◆———————

Amy and Oliver marry on January 3, 1917 at the First Parish, the Old Ship. The announcement runs two days later—it is restrained, even for our family.

Ferris – Litchfield

A quiet wedding was solemnized at the First Parish church, Wednesday evening at 6 o'clock by the Rev. H. Houghton Schumacher, the pastor.

The contracting parties were Miss Amy Litchfield, daughter of the late Wilbur T. and Frances Briggs Litchfield, and Mr. Oliver Morgan Ferris, son of Mr. and Mrs. Morgan E. Ferris, both of Hingham.

Only immediate relatives of the couple attended. They will reside in Hingham Centre.

—*Hingham Journal*, Jan. 5, 1917

In a photograph taken to mark their engagement or wedding, Oliver is handsome in a dark suit, vest, white shirt, and black bow tie. Amy, looking oh-so young, wears a tall hat embellished with buttons, a white ruffle collar blouse and a wide-striped skirt. Their expressions are serious. To smile in a photo would be indecorous.

The Last Baby, The Last Bride

After the wedding, Oliver moves into the house on School Street with Amy and her mother, aunt, and sister. Very soon, there is another female in the house, a baby girl. She is born to Amy at the end of March, less than three months after her marriage. Now, we understand the "quiet wedding."

The baby is named Barbara for a reason only my grandmother would know. She is the last baby born in the house, and she lives but nine days. Dr. Peterson gives "premature birth, gastritis" as the cause of death. A few early snowdrops may be placed on the tiny coffin before it is lowered into the ground, but in New England, the world is brown and bare at the beginning of April. They place no gravestone, no marker at all. She will be a secret and they will keep it. Barbara's siblings—my father, aunt, and uncle—will never know they had an older sister who died in infancy. No one will know outside of those who are there in 1917. Not until I remember something, something my grandmother Amy told me, unknowingly, when I was very young.

The week Barbara dies, America enters World War I. Neutrality has become impossible. American troops are deployed. Men register with the Selective Service. Oliver Ferris' record shows he is a married twenty-three-year-old carpenter with brown hair, blue eyes, and a slender build. He is not drafted and, hastened by America's involvement, the war ends a year and a half later. By then, Amy and Oliver have a second child, a son, my father. He is born in a hospital in Boston.

In September, the Spanish flu hits Massachusetts. Ruth, just two years out of nursing school, works throughout the crisis. The Boston area is hit hard. Schools, theaters, and even churches close in an effort to stop the spread of the disease. More than 45,000 people in the state die between September 1918 and January 1919. Fear is widespread; Amy and Oliver's baby is only a few months old. It's terrifying, but if anyone in the School Street household gets sick, they recover.

Ruth remains calm; she has a cool head like her mother and grandmother. She is in love, she sees the other side, and on May 31, 1919, she marries George Marsh, a fine artist and talented advertising executive, "at the home of the bride's mother." A minister of the First Parish, the Old Ship, performs the service. Family and friends attend. It is the last family wedding held in the house. Ruth is the last bride.

1917, the last baby. 1919, the last bride. The world changes as we watch.

Frances Makes up Her Mind

In 1919, Martha marries Eugene Skinner, an old friend of her late husband Rozy's, and moves to his house, leaving Frances with a dilemma. She now owns two houses—the one at number 74 in which she has a sole life estate and the one at number 68, which she inherited from her husband Wilbur and which is rented because she can't afford to live in it. Both of the houses are paid for, but Frances has no income, and taxes, utilities, maintenance, insurance, food, and medical bills all require cash. She comes up with a solution. First, she has Ruth, Amy, and their husbands legally sign over any interest they might have in the house at number 74 where she lives with Amy and her family. Then, she moves the renters at number 68 out so Ruth and George can move in. It looks simple, each daughter has a house, and each house has a wage earner. Legally it's not all that clean, but we won't think about that for years to come.

Although the family shares in the nation's optimism, the dance clubs, flapper dresses, and car culture of the Roaring Twenties have little relevance to the School Street households. Frances is a grandmother; Ruth and Amy both have children. Her sons-in-law have work. George is a rising star in the world of advertising, and while Oliver moves from situation to situation—shipyard laborer, carpenter, grocery store clerk—he always has a job. Then, in 1928, George gets a job offer from an advertising firm in Oakland, California. California? It is an enormous distance away, a huge distance to travel with small children, but they go. Number 68 is rented again. There is no thought of selling it. It is a family property, and when Ruth and George come home in the depths of the depression, it is there for them.

The Great Depression

On October 29, 1929, the stock market crashes, sparking a depression that will last more than ten years. It is the deepest financial crisis the country has known. The news reaches the School Street household by word of mouth. They do not have a radio, but a number of their neighbors do. The news is relentless. Banks fail, unemployment skyrockets, and houses and savings are lost. Anyone who does have money is afraid to spend it.

Frances adapts by expanding the household. Her widowed mother, Charlotte Briggs, moves in, and she takes in a boarder, Alonzo Osborne, a sixty-nine-year-old realtor. Her daughter Amy, her husband, and their three children, who are eight, ten, and eleven, are here. Her son-in-law, Oliver, is employed; he works for his father Morgan as a carpenter. However, the construction business is about to crash, putting them both out of work.

Every nook and cranny of the house is in use, and for the first time, food is a problem. This has always been a house of abundance, but it's not a farm anymore. The women plant vegetables and corn and tend the apple trees and berry bushes. They reinforce the hen house against raccoons. They can tomatoes, bake beans, and make casseroles from eggs, onions, and cabbage. They roast chestnuts and make jam if they have sugar. Potatoes and anything else in the kitchen become soup.

Eventually, the Government steps in with federal programs to put unemployed men back to work, and Oliver gets a job with the Work Projects Administration on local construction projects. It is the beginning of a return to normalcy, but it will be years before anything like plenty returns. My father, uncle, and aunt—Amy and Oliver's children—will remember this as adults. They are adolescents during the long depression, and they remember being hungry. Later, I am shocked to discover that when the boys, Richard and Morg, enter the Army at twenty and twenty-three years old, they weigh 135 and 134 pounds. Richard, my uncle, explains when I wonder about how thin they were then. "Times were hard," he says. "There was very little food."

The depression years take a toll on the house that will never really be reversed. It takes on the sheen of genteel poverty. On the grounds, the things that have fallen into disuse are coming apart. The woodshed is decaying. The carriage house is here, but it will fall in the next few years. I hear later, from my mother, that Oliver never showed much interest in the house. Maybe, I think, it is because he doesn't really see it as his house, full of women as it is. Or maybe it's because he works all day as a carpenter and has no desire to take it up at home. Maybe, as it is said, he likes a drink, or maybe he just likes his life—his work, the men at the fire station, the weekend ball games, his newspaper at night. Maybe, he just doesn't need the weight of all that history. His wife, Amy Trowbridge Litchfield Ferris, can wear that mantle.

There are two deaths on School Street during the depression. In November 1938, Oliver's father Morgan dies of a heart attack at home at number 45. He is seventy-eight. It is sudden. The news travels across the village. On the Monday, funeral services are held at his house. A minister of the First Baptist Church offici-ates. Someone tells this story that day, probably his son Oliver because he was there. It is fall. Morgan and Oliver are shingling a roof on Middle Street to the sounds of the high school football game. As the cheers grow louder and excitement pulses, Morgan, an avid sports fan, can take no more. He lays down his hammer and level, climbs down the ladder and, without a word to anyone, including the startled homeowner, takes off at a sprint for the game. The roof is left to be finished another day. They all laugh. It is legend. They bury him, the exuberant Irishman, in the Centre cemetery, a lifetime away from Ireland, miles from the Catholic cemetery where his sister Hannah is buried, but close to his home on School Street where he lived for forty-four years. His wife Annie will be buried next to him, and all three of their children will be buried nearby.

Two years later, Frances' mother, Charlotte Gardner Briggs, dies in number 74, the old Cushing homestead, where she has lived for thirty years. History says she was a teacher and a shoe-maker before she married William Briggs, who was sixteen years her senior, and had three children. Her granddaughter says she was an expert gardener and attended the Quaker church. Her great-grandson says her "claim to fame" is that she shook hands with Abraham Lincoln "on one of his swings through the state." Her obituary writer says, "She was in her 99th year and reported to be Hingham's oldest resident."

Funeral services are private and held at home in the house on School Street. A minister of the Old Ship Church officiates.

1940, the last funeral.

War

The depression wanes as war looms. Some say only the war effort will finally lift it. Oliver gets a job at the Museum of Fine Arts in Boston as a cabinetmaker. The offer comes to him through a man he met while he was working for the Works Project Admin-istration. Mornings, he walks to the Square, stops at the diner for a nickel cup of coffee, and catches the train to work. He reads the paper as the world streams by. There is a war being fought in Europe. America is reluctant to enter, but there is concern that the nation will soon have to defend itself against the rising threats of Germany and Japan. His sons Morg and Richard, grown now, are talking about it. The war. The National Guard. The Army. The Air Corps.

The U.S. Navy turns its attention to Hingham. Small town that it is, Hingham is already an international target. For out there in west Hingham, on all those acres of farmland the Navy bought in the early 1900s, is located an ammunition depot. The torpedoes and ammunition stored there supply the Atlantic Fleet. But more space is needed and in 1941, the Navy proposes the construction of an ammunition annex on Union Street in the Third Division Woods. It will be a mile from the house on School Street. Public input is taken, but despite concerns and protests, the seven-square mile facility is built. Bombs and other high explosives are moved to the site, and a railroad spur is constructed to haul ammunition between the annex and the depot at the shipyard. Fear lives close to home.

In December 1941, the Japanese bomb the U.S. Pacific Fleet at anchor in Hawaii, and the country enters World War II. All men between the ages of 18 and 65 register with the Selective Service. Richard, twenty, enlists. Morg, twenty-three, registers; he will be drafted. Oliver, himself, is forty-seven, unlikely to be called, but he fills out a registration card, providing a phone number—Hingham 1354M—so we know there is a telephone in the house. It is a heavy black rotary dial model that sits on a small telephone table at the bottom of the back stairs. It, or one like it, will be there for decades, falling into disuse eventually—people stop calling when my grandmother Amy can no longer hear it ring. But that is forty years in the future.

It's impossible to miss the increased military presence in

town, and when the Navy opens a shipyard on Hewitt's Cove in 1942, workers pour in from neighboring towns. During the day, Hingham's population of 8,000 skyrockets—by the end of 1942, the shipyard employs 15,000, and in 1943, 24,000 workers are on hand to build and launch the destroyer escorts that the Navy has ordered.

Military guards patrol the town. Men and women alike take jobs at the depots and shipyard. Oliver becomes a volunteer Air Warden, enforcing the blackout. Rationing is enacted. Families buy war bonds. Children collect used blankets, old tires, garden hoses, and tin cans. Victory gardens are planted; a canning center opens at Agricultural Hall. Ruth works as a nurse. Both she and Amy volunteer with the Red Cross. They roll bandages, knit socks, and hold benefits. Ruth drives them to work parties and meetings in her car. Amy will never have a car; she will never learn to drive.

The war officially ends on September 2, 1945, and soon it is chaotic on School Street. It's hard to believe the boys Morg and Richard are home—Guam, Australia, Hawaii, so far away they have been, places previously only read about in books and atlases. The house is crowded again, but it's not the same because, unlike the old days, all of this is temporary. Not one of Amy and Oliver's children will stay home. They want houses of their own, and they will get them in the next chapter—the last chapter of this story. They come and go, camping out now and then when they are between houses and visiting on the holidays and Sundays, but they are all moving on. A new wind is blowing through the old house.

The Matriarch is Dead, Long Live the Matriarch

Quiet descends on the house. Only Frances, Amy, and Oliver are at home. Amy has gone to work as a librarian in the children's room. It is a short distance to the public library, and she walks five days a week in rain, snow, or oppressive heat dressed in a print dress, stockings, stack-heeled lace-up oxfords, and a sweater or coat. Her handbag rests over her forearm, and she wears a hat secured with a hatpin. Skidmore would be proud of its "girl."

Monday through Friday, Oliver puts on his fedora and walks to the train station. On the weekends if he is not at the ballgame, he is at the firehouse, playing checkers and talking to the fraternity of men who gather there. Frances, in her seventies, is home alone during the day. She gardens and cooks. She attends meetings of the Arts and Crafts Society. She babysits for her great-grandchildren. One winter she notices that the cold bothers her more, and she moves next door to Ruth's where the upstairs is heated. In the spring and summer, she is back at number 74 in her old room, the southwest chamber. It is just a walk across a lawn.

Frances is in her eighties when Amy and Ruth start to worry. She is having a harder time with the stairs. She forgets. She leaves the teakettle on, the side door wide open. They care for her and we, her great-grandchildren, are enlisted to stop by after school and check on her. We play cards and answer her questions about school. I'm sure we are unsatisfactory conversationalists, and today I regret every question I didn't ask, but I am twelve and thirteen; I don't even know what questions to ask. Then one day she falls and fractures her femur, or perhaps the bone is so brittle it splinters when she stands. Amy and Ruth agree their mother is too fragile for them to care for. She must go to a nursing home. They find a place close by where gradually, her heart slows and she dies on March 3, 1961. She is eighty-nine years old. Her obituary, which runs in the *Hingham Journal* on March 9, refers to her as Mrs. Wilbur T. Litchfield, although she has been a widow for fifty years. Her funeral is not held at home on School Street, but at a funeral parlor.

Mrs. Wilbur T. Litchfield

Frances (Briggs) Litchfield, 89, of 74 School Street, Hingham Center, wife of the late Wilbur T. Litchfield, died on Friday at a Norwell nursing home after a long illness. She had lived in Hingham for nearly 70 years . . . She was a former member of the Hingham Arts and Crafts Society . . .

Private funeral services were held from the Downing Cottage Chapel, Pond street, Hingham Center on Sunday afternoon. The Rev. Donald F. Robinson of the Second Parish Church officiated at the rites. Burial was in the Hingham Center Cemetery.

And she is gone, my great-grandmother. I am fourteen. Children are not allowed to go to the funeral. It is private and for adults. We don't question such a directive, but I miss her. When I am in the house after she is gone, her empty upstairs rooms weigh heavy over me. We only go to the second floor to use the bathroom, but then, I peer into every room, remembering the big beds, the trunks, the shiny little things, the old dresses, the books. Soon all the rooms are empty, even the pulley clothesline that ran from the window in the back bedroom to a tree in the yard is gone. Such a magical thing it was to reel in the line, pin slips, socks, and dresses on it and reel it out again to watch the laundry flap in the wind.

We called Frances "Muchie," no one knows why. The sadness comes to me in a dream. I am lost in her rooms upstairs. She was kind; she was unhurried when everyone else was busy. We picked apples together from a rickety wooden ladder, and I snuggled next to her on the couch while she read the newspaper. But it was also she who taught me, as did my mother and my grandmother, that we don't cry out, we don't call attention to ourselves for some hurt. But I know where she is buried and I go there.

I know, now, where they are all buried.

The Eighth Owners

Following their mother Frances' death, Amy and Ruth become the eighth owners of the house at 74 School Street. They also inherit the house at number 68, the one their father Wilbur built in 1896. Indeed, together they hold all of the land that the Colonel did when he built his house in the summer of 1785.

Amy and Ruth. Ruth and Amy. While they have lived with each other or next door to each other for most of their lives, and they are unmistakably sisters—good mothers and kind, soft-spoken, wise women—the differences between them have long been evident. Amy is a homebody, a dreamer, a reader, where Ruth, a visiting nurse, a church volunteer, and a Girl Scout leader, is a practical force in the community. Their personalities are, of course, different. Amy is younger and shyer, but maybe more significantly, she has been for all of her life, the youngest woman in a house of women, content to let the elders make the decisions. Except, of course, in love. She had her own way when it came to love.

After Frances dies, Amy and Oliver live alone for the first time in their married lives. They are sixty-six and sixty-seven years old. The house settles deeper into the earth, and the spirits knock about. The floorboards warp and the ancient electric wiring blinks in the wind. The pantry off the back of the kitchen lists to one side and fills with clay pots, spider webs, and odds and ends. The upstairs is empty; there are no more overnight guests. The attic still harbors the old spinning wheel and the embroidery samplers of times gone by, but we never go up there anymore. We are teenagers and young adults, and we sit in the front parlor where there is a fire in the fireplace and where the sun and moon rise and set across the top of the grandfather clock that stands in the corner where it has stood for many years since Frances first brought it to the house. African violets collect dust on a plant stand near the front window, blooming erratically.

At number 68 Ruth and George are also at home alone, their children grown. Ruth maintains the place in spick-and-span readiness, as if someone is coming at any moment. Cut flowers reflect in highly polished tables, the kitchen is clean and tidy. There is banana bread on the counter and jewel-tone jars of jam line the pantry shelves. Her children come to visit and bring their children, but everyone has their own home. I come because she teaches me to sew and lets me use the sewing machine in her bedroom to make the clothes I wear in high school. She teaches me about interfacing and shows me how to place a zipper. She knows how to cut a pattern more efficiently than any diagram and how to sew an invisible hem. How this came to be, I don't know, but my mother and grandmother don't sew. My mother says she didn't learn, and my grandmother has given it up and retreated to her books. Thankfully, Aunt Ruth teaches me this and much more.

———◆———

Oliver suffers "a long illness" and retires. He dies at seventy, at home in the house on School Street on an early morning in March 1965. An obituary reports that he graduated from Hingham High, worked as a cabinetmaker for the Museum of Fine Arts, and was a member of the Old Ship Church. A service is held at a funeral parlor; there are no visiting hours. I see that we have become more private. The sociability of Roswell, Sarahlane, Sarah, Martha, Rozy, and Wilbur is gone. The days of throwing open the house are gone. We don't have big wakes at home anymore or large afternoon socials or progressive dinners or church benefits. We are more reserved. Have we changed or have the times? Do the poverty years of the great depression worry us still, or has the rise of radios, grocery stores, funeral parlors, movie theaters, and cars made us more insular like everyone else?

There are a dozen or more photos of Oliver, seated behind his open newspaper, walking home along School Street, and holding a baby, but I have only one letter. He wrote it to my father, who he calls Brud, a version of Brother, while he was at summer camp with his brother Richard. It is in the middle of the depression. He worries about rain and food.

Sunday July 9, '33

Dear Brud,
I suppose by this time you are able to swim the length of the pond. Did you & Richard get in the same tent? Who are the other boys in your tent. Ken came down & said he might go to camp the last two weeks. I suppose you eat like a horse. If you boys go on an overnight hike be sure to take *raincoats* & not lay on the damp ground, tell Richard to do the same. Have you seen John or any other of the boys from

Hingham. I was going in to the ball game today but it rained & I didn't go. Do they have any boxing bouts or wrestling. Drop me a line in time to let us know how you are coming home. Keep an eye on Richard—eat so much you will gain about ten pounds. Well as you know there is nothing exciting so I will close. Drop us a line—tell me all the exciting things you are doing. Try & pass some of your tests. Hoping to hear from you soon. Dad.

Oliver is buried in the cemetery at the Centre. Amy will be buried next to him. Their graves are across the cemetery from the rest of the family. Why this is, I don't know.

Amy is home alone. She will live here by herself for the next twenty-four years. She is the only one who has ever lived alone in the house. She reads, knits, and cares for her cats. She adopts every stray that wanders by until someone calls an animal rescue organization to come and pick them up. They leave her one or two and soon a few more have found their way to her doorstep. She joins the Golden Age Club and goes on bus trips. She plays cards with her friends but, one by one, they die. She watches the Red Sox on her portable black-and-white TV. She fills the bird feeders. She visits with Ruth. She walks to the movie theater at night. One day I hear a neighbor ask her if she isn't afraid to walk downtown in the dark, the streetlights being few.

"Oh, no," she says. "Not at all."

"What if you run into Joe?" the woman persists, referring to the tall rangy man we kids know as 'Old Joe,' the town drunk.

"Oh, my," says my grandmother, "there is no one I would rather see of a night than Joe. He always steps off the sidewalk, tips his hat, and says, 'Good evening, Mrs. Ferris.'"

My opinion of my grandmother and Old Joe change that day. A gray-haired grandma unafraid of the dark? A polite drunk? That is something to think about. Of course, I don't know then that my grandmother has known Joe since he was a little boy, and that she knew his mother and probably his grandmother. No, I don't know all that, and it will be a long time before I do.

The End of the Line

In 1971 Amy and Ruth are seventy-six and seventy-eight years old. Their mother Frances has been dead ten years, and they have not yet sorted out their inheritance—they jointly own both houses. Ruth decides it's time to take action, and they have the land surveyed. They each keep the house they live in and some land around them, but they sell off about two-and-a-half acres at the back of the property. Their land no longer runs to the river.

The end is in sight.

———◆———

On a cold night at the beginning of January 1989, Amy goes to bed early with a cold. She takes off her glasses, folds them on top of her book, and goes to sleep for the last time. She is ninety-three. It is her seventy-second wedding anniversary. Does she dream of her Oliver on this last night, the boy she fell in love with? Do the old memories swirl about her? Do they visit her, the house spirits? My uncle finds her in the morning. The undertaker comes for her.

The death certificate says she died of heart disease. I might say she died on her anniversary because she was ever the romantic—the "True Lover" of her school yearbook—and because she was ready to follow her blue-eyed boy. And that might have been.

Amy Litchfield Ferris
Retired Librarian

Private services for Amy T. (Litchfield) Ferris, 93, of Hingham were held at Downing Cottage Funeral Chapel. Burial also was private.

Mrs. Ferris died Jan. 3 at home after a brief illness.

Born in Hingham, she was a lifelong resident. She attended local schools, Skidmore College at Saratoga Springs, N.Y., and Bridgewater Normal School.

She was a librarian in the children's department at Hingham Public Library for more than 20 years, retiring in 1965. She was a member of the Hingham Golden Age Club . . .

Visiting hours and flowers are to be omitted by request.

Donations in memory of Mrs. Ferris may be made to the Hingham Public Library, 66 Leavitt St., Hingham.

—*Hingham Journal,* Jan. 5, 1989

———————◄•►———————

Ruth lives three years longer than her sister. She has been widowed a number of years. "Bad knees," she complains, force her into a wheelchair and a nursing home. The house is sold. She has no illusion that she will come home. Dismantling the house is arduous. She gives my mother the cut glass punch bowl, which sat for so many years in the dining room and which had come to her from her Uncle Rozy and Aunt Martha who had received it as a gift for their twenty-fifth wedding anniversary. She writes in a note to my mother that she has heard the house at number 68 looks "awful without the furniture & pictures," and goes on to say, "I'm not worrying about the leaves—the new owners will have to do that." It breaks my heart to read this note, because she misses that house. On the one hand, she may not be unhappy that the house looks "awful" without her possessions in it, on the other hand, despite what she says, she is worried about the leaves.

When my mother and I visit her in the nursing home, she tells us that the day she signed the papers to sell the house at number 68, the one her father Wilbur built, was the saddest day of her life. She lives to a venerable age and dies in the hospital in which she nursed. She is buried with her husband, parents, and the ancestors in the cemetery at the Centre.

Ruth Marsh, 97, nurse, honorary Hingham VNA member

HINGHAM – Ruth (Litchfield) Marsh of Hingham, an honorary member of the Hingham Visiting Nurse Association, died yesterday at South Shore Hospital.

Mrs. Marsh was born in Hingham. She was a graduate of Brookline High School and attended New England Baptist School of Nursing.

She was a nurse in Hingham during the flu epidemic of 1918.

Mrs. Marsh was active in the Women's Alliance at Old Ship Church.

She was a Girl Scout leader many years and a volunteer at South Shore Hospital . . . A memorial service will be held at 3 p.m. Friday at Downing Cottage Funeral Chapel, 21 Pond St. Burial in Hingham Center Cemetery will be private.

There are no visiting hours. Donations may be made to the Hingham Visiting Nurse Association, 10 Downer Ave., Hingham 02043.

—*Hingham Journal,* Jan. 31, 1991

   The house at number 68 is remodeled and updated. It's lonely, knowing her roll-top desk in no longer in the living room, that Uncle George's oil paintings are no longer on the walls. And anyone passing by can see that her garden and flowerbeds are gone.

Really, it is all gone.

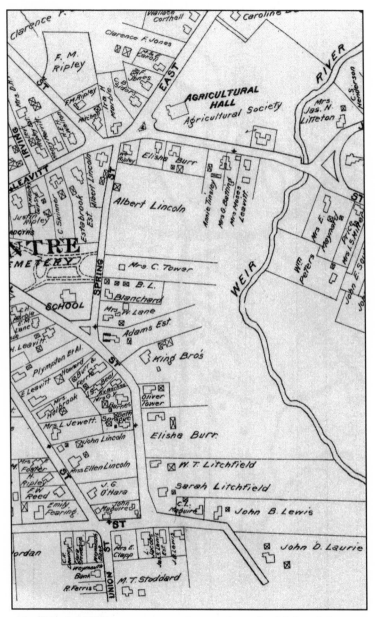

The Litchfield homes are at the south end of School Street.
The Ferris home is near the intersection of Spring Street.

Three generations: Rita Ferris, Amy Litchfield Ferris, and the author, Meg Ferris Kenagy.

Chapter 11

The Sellers, 1989

*People today are so busy trying to keep up with the
Joneses, they don't visit with people like they used
to, especially with their families. Life is too fast.*

—Morg Ferris, my father, circa 1980

Amy Trowbridge Litchfield Ferris, the eighth owner of the
house at 74 School Street, dies at home in January 1989. She is
ninety-three. The house is 204 and from the road, it looks like
another white Colonial. It is only if you look closely that you see
the damp patches rising from the foundation and notice the peel-
ing paint. Then you see the lilacs are leggy and the flower gardens
are tangled with weeds. If you are from one of the old families,
you probably miss these things because the house is so familiar
to you. You may not even notice the carriage house is gone. If you
are an old timer, you might even see the barn and smell the pigs.

———————◆◆———————

If she ever thinks about it, Amy knows she is the last of the
family to live in the house; her children have their own lives.

People—younger neighbors and relatives—wonder that she lives alone in her nineties, but for her there is nothing to fear in the house. To her, I'm quite sure, the house has never truly been empty. The many lives that have passed through it shimmer still. She is not afraid of intruders either, although some think she should be. The side door is unlocked for the better part of 170 years because there is no lock on it until one day someone decides there should be and my father installs one. My mother worries that at night Amy has to cross the house and go up the narrow back stairs to the bathroom. What if she falls? But Amy remains unperturbed.

When she is ninety years old, Amy writes her will, or rather, she changes her will. The story is this. Three months after my father dies at age sixty-six, my mother stops to visit Amy and bring her dinner. On her way in the door, she meets Amy's lawyer on his way out; he is a neighbor. The women have a visit, but Amy says nothing about the lawyer's call. Later, my mother tells one of her friends the story, wondering if her mother-in-law Amy has changed her will because my father died. "Of course, she did," says her friend. "These old Yankees are going to make sure the house stays in the bloodline." Her friend is an old Yankee herself. Telling me the story after the fact, my mother, the Irish Catholic, laughs and shrugs. "I have no idea what Grammy will do."

The lovely thing is that Amy does change her will, leaving the house to her two living children and the widow of her deceased son, my mother, "in equal shares and as tenants in common."

———◆———

Amy and Oliver's children, Morg, Marjorie, and Richard, the last generation to grow up in the house on School Street, are children in the 1920s, teenagers and young adults during the depression.

In 1930, there are so many people in the house—their parents, grandmother, great-grandmother, and a boarder—that rooms have to be rearranged. Their parents convert the dining room to a bedroom and move the table into the smaller room off the kitchen that once served as the Colonel's office. Morg and Richard, twelve and nine years old, sleep in the old birthing room at the end of the kitchen where two narrow bunks have been built. Upstairs, Marjorie, eleven, has a bed in the small storage closet off her grandmother Frances' room. Their great-grandmother Charlotte and the boarder each have one of the other two upstairs rooms. The one small bathroom—toilet, sink, and claw-foot bathtub—is never enlarged.

They make do. These years are etched in my father's memory. He has two jobs during high school: a paper route and a job at a local dairy. Every day, he brings in the cows and cleans the barn and dairy. Every day, he delivers milk and newspapers. He will say later that the depression taught him the value of a dollar, a lesson he never forgot.

He graduates from high school in 1937. He is handsome and serious in his graduation photo. He works that summer, and in the fall, he enters a three-year course in wood-patternmaking at Wentworth Institute in Boston.

My Father Marries a Girl from out of Town

My father loves jazz, and on the weekends, he and his friends go into Boston to the clubs. On this particular night in 1939, when he is twenty-one, they are at the Raymor-Playmor Ballroom where the big bands come to play—Benny Goodman, Jack Teagarden, Helen O'Connell, and Jimmy and Tommy Dorsey. My mother, Rita Scanlan, is there with her cousin Mary. My father asks my mother to dance. It is the beginning of their story. He asks for her phone number. He meets her Irish Catholic parents, which doesn't go well. He is a Protestant, a member of the First Parish, the Old Ship. Her parents are opposed to the relationship. My mother's mother softens a little on the day my father cuts his visit with my mother short because he has to pick up his mother and grandmother at the movies and drive them home. "Well, it sounds like he's good to his mother," she relents. But her father won't be happy until my father leaves the First Parish and becomes a Catholic, which he will do to marry my mother.

When he graduates from Wentworth, my father gets a job with a manufacturer in South Boston earning $26 a week. This is where Uncle Sam finds him. Under time pressure, he and my mother set a wedding date of April 25. On April 19, a letter arrives at the house on School Street, instructing him to report for service in ten days. The wedding goes on. The photos are black-and-white snapshots taken in the backyard of my mother's house in Dorchester. My mother is radiant in a white dress and frothy veil she claims she "wasn't wild about," but that her older sister has chosen. My father, handsome and happy in tails, poses with everyone, and here are the School Street women: Frances Litchfield, grandmother of the groom, in a long black dress with beautiful detailing and a hat with a large flower and Amy Litchfield Ferris, mother of the groom, in a floral print knee-length dress with a ruffle around the neck and a wide-brimmed hat.

The newlyweds go to New Hampshire for a few days, and then my father reports to Fort Devens to be inducted into the Army. My mother stays at home with her parents and siblings. She works in the payroll department of a metal parts manufacturer. My father is inducted, inoculated, and the teeth he is missing due to lack of dental care during the depression are replaced. He is trained in aircraft mechanics and sent to Hawaii and then Guam to work on the fighter planes that bomb Japan.

Their wedding announcement runs in the *Hingham Journal*

five days later, but my father doesn't see it. He is in basic training. The headline, "Oliver L. Ferris weds Dorchester girl" is worthy of note. It says that a Hingham man has married a 24-year-old "girl" from Boston's Irish Catholic neighborhood.

———————◆◆———————

In the fall of 1943, my mother takes the train to Hingham to visit her in-laws. She brings a small notebook so family and neighbors can write a note to my father. She and Amy walk down the street, visiting along the way, gathering comments. (My father, who my mother and his friends call Morg, is also called Brother, Brud, and Oliver. The nicknames are necessary because both his father and his grandfather are named Oliver.) Here are the School Street entries.

> Dear Brud, The best of health, of luck and God's speed to the senior member of my two man Air Force. Dad (Oliver Ferris)

> Dear Brother, I am in the habit of writing V-mail and so it seems strange to write in a book. Rita showed us those snaps taken on your picnic and they were swell. You look in the pink of condition. Mother (Amy Litchfield Ferris)

> Sunday Oct 31, 1943. Dear Brother, 'Pop' and Stevie and Jay and I have just returned from a walk to Turkey Hill. It was beautiful—the oaks were a hill ant red against the blue water. I expect your colors are much more intense that ours. Hoping to see you before many moons – Love Aunt Ruth (Ruth Litchfield Marsh)

Hello, Oliver, How are you making out, got any Japs yet? How is chances for me starting a little milk route out there? Your wife and your old Mom are here at the moment to get my testimony. (A neighbor and dairyman)

Nov 6th 1943. My Dear Grandson Oliver, How are you feeling now-a-days. If you feel as good as you look with that nice little mustache of yours, I bet you cut quite a dash. I like it very much and you know I, being the glamour girl of School St., should know all about those things. We were all so happy to hear you were feeling so well and hope to see you soon. There is never a day or night but you are with us in thought and we are wondering first where you are and how you are doing, so always keep that in mind. Lots of love from all, your loving Grandma Ferris and Uncle Gordon. XXXXXXXX (Annie Tower Ferris)

And I fall in love with my great-grandmother Annie, Morgan's widow, who I don't remember because she died in 1948 when I was a year and a half old. Who wouldn't want to have known "the glamour girl of School Street" with all her love and kisses? A sharp contrast to my father's mother and father, who signed simply, "Dad" and "Mother."

———◆———

The war officially ends in September 1945, and Morg and Richard are discharged on the Army's schedule—decommissioning the military is a huge task. Their sister Marjorie is at home, she will soon marry a Coast Guard seaman, and he will move into the house. My mother and father will also move in, taking over the northwest chamber that was once Martha's. Richard is engaged, and after he marries, he and his wife will move into the house for a time. Frances, Amy, and Oliver are at home, but the house does what it has always done, makes room, takes in, expands.

Then there are babies in the house again, hospital babies. My cousin Susan is born in the spring, I am born in the fall. My uncle tells me later, that we were spoiled, that all the women spoiled us, and probably they did. But then everyone is leaving. The post-war generation is moving on. The economic boom has promised everyone a job, a house, a car, and a road to drive it on. Refrigerators, TVs, and washing machines are all part of the dream. We baby boomers toddle into a new world. The Golden Age of Capitalism is born.

Amy and Oliver's Grandchildren

There are twelve of us in this the last generation of School Street kids. My father has seven, Marjorie has four, and Richard, one. We visit our grandparents. There is the chaos of Christmas morning, ten girls and two boys. We come at Thanksgiving to sit at the round table in the dining room and at Halloween to trick-or-treat. On May Day, we leave crepe-paper baskets of violets or pansies on the front door. We play cards and dress up in long dresses pulled from our great-grandmother's trunks. We venture into the attic with its out-of-sight rustlings. We listen to the radio. Grammy makes brownies and chocolate cake with marshmallow frosting. We watch the fire snap and crackle in the parlor fireplace. We swing on an old rope swing in the backyard and climb the apple trees. We run up the front stairs and down the back and gaze suspiciously at the old high tank pull chain toilet.

We grow up, the dozen of us. We go away to school, find jobs, get married. We bring our babies to visit, then our children. Later, when my grandmother lives alone, we come to wash the curtains or to bring her dinner and to sit in the front parlor and visit. We bring books; we play with the cats.

The house is an antique. An electric stove sits next to the old black stove. There is a relic of a washing machine at the end of the kitchen but no dryer. The wood floors are warped. The kitchen floor slopes noticeably downhill. My younger sisters recall the upstairs rooms as all but empty of furniture, and one of them remembers going upstairs one day to find the sole wooden rocking chair in the back bedroom rocking slowly back and forth.

———◆———

The town is a residential community. New families move in; new houses are built. Coffee shops, nail salons, and upscale restaurants open. The old farmhouses are remodeled or torn down. My father laments the loss of community. He finds things to applaud: modern heat (he knows the cold of an unheated house), appliances, social programs, and better public transportation, but he misses the Hingham Centre community. Late in his life he writes, "Life in the 20th century has been very fast for me. Growing up, school, war, marriage, family." And for him it is, he dies at sixty-six.

His brother Richard, who upholds the family commitment to firefighting as a lieutenant in the Hingham fire department, also laments the loss of community. He will live to be ninety-five, and he will be amazed when all of the old families are gone from the Centre, the families that had been there for generations. He will shake his head in disbelief, "All gone, not one original family left."

———◆———

I am born into this story in 1946, one of the first baby boomers. This is when I meet Amy, Oliver, and Frances—my grandmother, grandfather, and great-grandmother—or more precisely when they meet me. My memories of them begin later, growing from blurry vignettes to vivid snapshots to remembered conversations. This is also where my relationship to the house and the land is born. And after all the years and all the miles—I am Thursday's child and, as the old nursery rhyme goes, I do have far to go—I still remember the house as it was then, its smell of vanilla and nuts, old wood, old books.

I remember standing on a chair next to my grandmother at the sink, washing strawberries. I remember the purple drapes with the tattered linings on the four-poster bed upstairs and how they moved in the dark and rustled in the breeze from the open window. I remember pinning clothes on the line from a wooden stool. I remember the flower garden and following my grandmother Amy as she knelt on the ground with a trowel. I remember the birds. I remember my great-grandmother Frances turning over weeds and dirt with her pitchfork. At night, I remember listening to the house, its creaking and sighing. The old wood popping. Is that rustling a squirrel in the attic or a bird in the chimney?

It is quiet in that early world. So much comes and goes around me, so many women in silky dresses and aprons, women I know and women I don't know. Later there is laughter and noise, card games, and TV shows, but my deepest earliest memories are encased in safety and quiet, surrounded by women.

———————◼◆◼———————

There is a photo of me with my grandparents taken in front of the house. The afternoon sun casts shadows. I am a year and some months old. They are exactly as I remember them. My grandmother in a print dress with a matching belt, nylons, and black stack-heeled shoes. Her stance is solid; no breeze shakes this woman. My grandfather is inscrutable in a suit and tie and hat. I am a sturdy wispy-haired blond toddler in a jacket and pants, clinging to their hands, my face turned away from the sun. We are all serious; no one shouts "smile" in these days. More likely I have been told to stand still.

I don't remember that day, but I remember many others. Normal days that play in my memory in slow motion, which is how they must have unfolded. Curious days, the shimmery past, what was real? Who are the women in my dreams and in those hazy moments in time? Did some collective memory swirl there in the side garden and as the birds moved to ancient rhythms, did we bow to ancient memory? Where really does memory live? Can it not be present in a room or a lilac bush or on a breeze through an old house? Can it not be locked in a spinning wheel or a beloved book? I don't know, but it could be. Maybe it was the stories my grandmother Amy, great-grandmother Frances, and Aunt Ruth told that ignited my imagination. Maybe Martha was there. Martha of the long white dresses. I was three years old when she died. I don't know, but I am content to have sought out these women and to have given them the voices I could.

And what do I see in the long journey? I see immigrants who help build a town and participate in its government. I see how religion shapes lives and that hard work is a religion of its own. I see that community, home, and land are to be revered. I see women who care for their families and find ways to help others while they contend with illness, loss, and prejudice. I see men who find work when there is little work to be found and who always work. I see room is made for change, and that grief and loss are always part of the fabric of family. I see men who die young and widowed women who raise children in the safety net of an old house, a place for which they fight mightily. I see money is spent on housing, education, and community. I see strength and faith, belief in nature and neighbor. I see where I am from.

Gone

The house is sold. The real estate flyer calls it an "unspoiled antique in strong location" and lists a number of features.

> 5 fireplaces
> In the same family for 8 generations
> Basement is partial with dirt floor
> Furnace does not adequately heat house
> Pine floors
> Birthing room
> 5 bedrooms
> 1 bath
> No landscaping

A family from out of town buys the house. It is gutted, enlarged, and landscaped. It is a beautiful house, but it is now someone else's house. I can't say I feel anything at all when, at an open house, I walk through the expanded bedrooms, gleaming bathrooms, gourmet kitchen, and large family room. I know immediately that the spirits are gone, and I sense nothing at all when I walk away, down the asphalt driveway that has buried the curved flowerbeds and taken the lilac hedge. There is no one here. They are gone. They were gone with my grandmother, the last of them to die in the old house. They were gone before she was laid with them in the cemetery. They were gone before the house was ripped back to its bones, revealing the timber post-and-beam construction. They were gone before the back walls of the house fell, before the swimming pool was dug or the decking installed, before some piece of machinery demolished the birthing room.

Why they came to me when I was a child and stayed with me, I don't know. It may be that I was a child who heard the house's comings and goings with a child's mind, early enough that the present and the past were different sides of the same coin.

It may also have been that they were growing restless, the home spirits, as if they knew the end of their line was near, and they were gathering—like birds for migration—and I was just there to bear witness.

Epilogue or How I Know About the Baby

My grandmother was born in 1895 into a Puritan family of the first water. Into a time and a place where the past was always present. She was a girl of the Old Church, the First Parish. She married the boy from down the street, the one she went to grammar school with. They had three children who went to the same schools they did, who married and had children of their own who went to the same schools.

To me, she was solid and soft at the same time, a woman of aprons and housecoats and silky print dresses. When she went out, she always wore a hat and a coat. Never did she wear lipstick or pants or jewelry. Her hair was a white curly halo, and she wore a gold wedding ring that was as thin as a whisper. She loved cats and babies, but she was shy with adults. A grandmother straight out of one of Norman Rockwell's paintings. But she had a secret, and she told it to me, unwittingly, when I was five or six. It was certainly because I was young that she told me. Who would expect a child to make something of such a small thing? Or to let it haunt her for decades until she went back and unearthed it, the secret?

———◆◆———

Amy Litchfield Ferris was fifty-one when I was born. She and my grandfather lived in the old house on School Street with her mother, Frances. The house smelled of sawdust and wood smoke and dry stuffed furniture and ancient books. I don't remember a time when my grandmother wasn't there. She was always there. My earliest memories are of sleeping with her in the big high bed. Of turning pages in a picture book. Of egg salad sandwiches and brownies and being outside in the garden. Of birds and tomatoes. Of flickering fireplaces that I was held back from. Of quiet. Of rain against the wavy old windowpanes. Of a bird book that had music notes in it.

When I was at her house, I followed her about, standing on a chair at the kitchen sink or dragging a rake as she worked in the gardens. I remember standing on a pitchfork once and how it slid into the earth under my weight, and how I trailed after her then pulling out weeds as she uncovered them. All around us was birdsong, and I felt beloved. She and I walked to the store and the library, her handle purse over her arm, her hand in mine. It was the 1950s, but we walked because there was not a car at that house, nor would there ever be a car at that house. We also walked to the cemetery to visit the family graves. It was just down the road—a leafy, quiet place. I had never been to a cemetery before I went with her, and just the two of us went. My parents were building their family, not burying it, and I never saw my grandfather walk through its iron gates.

But that cemetery! I knew from the first moment that I had been allowed into a secret place, a garden of stones. Many of them were leaning, partially buried and splattered with silvery-green lichen, their carved words fading. Some were planted flat in the ground, some rose like statues above me. I don't think I could read when I first went, because while I remember the winged angels of death, the carved flowers, and the strange letters with beautiful flourishes, I don't remember any words.

On one of these days—a cold one because I remember Grammy was wearing a long gray coat—she brought with us to the cemetery a small bunch of flowers in a white lacy paper doily. I didn't notice it until we had made our way over the uneven ground to the middle of the cemetery and she bent down and laid it on the brown grass.

"Who is that for?" I asked, unable to bear the thought of leaving such a beautiful little posy there on the bare ground.

"The baby," she said.

And she took my hand and we walked home to her house on School Street.

A dead baby left in the ground disturbed me. Babies were not to die and be left in a cemetery. I had two younger sisters, one a chubby baby with pink cheeks. Babies, I knew, were not to die. It worried me—I was already an anxious child—but not enough to stop me from going with her to the family graves. I went for a number of years, until I was a teenager, I suppose, and too busy for my grandmother. She planted spicy-smelling geraniums late in the spring and left the last roses of summer in green cardboard cones. But we never again went to where the baby was buried, and there was never another paper doily nosegay.

And I, well versed in the family liturgy of discretion and privacy, was too much of her granddaughter to ask why. I knew, even then, about boundaries and the mysteries of God's will and Puritan fate, which hung in that cemetery like early morning fog.

I went to college on the West Coast, married, and had children, but when I came home, I always saw my grandmother. By the time she was seventy, she lived alone in the big house, my grandfather dead and buried in our cemetery. The house was slowly settling around her. Electric cords frayed and sparked and damp patches rose up the side of the house as the stone foundation that had been laid in 1785 sank unevenly and deeper into the earth. The neglected gardens fell into a tangle of berries and briars, and the branches on the lilacs grew as thick as those of trees. Shingles were on the wind in every storm, and paint peeled in the sun. There was no money to shore things up, but no one dared suggest she leave the house. Her people did not leave the house. They died in the rooms they were born in.

For company in those years, Grammy had cats, baseball, and her books. She read one after another without regard to genre. A paper bag on one side of her chair was for unread books. A paper bag on the other accepted volumes to be returned to the Golden Age Club or the library. When I went to see her, my mother came with me. I was only home for a couple of weeks so what we did, we did together. Usually my mother unloaded the groceries we brought or washed up the dishes so I could visit with my grandmother. One summer day, we were talking about books, and I asked her if she were ever to write a book what she would write about.

"I'd write a Russian spy novel," she said without hesitation. "I could do better than most of them."

My mother came into the room in time to hear the answer and later as we were driving home, she said, "Well, I never! I've never heard Grammy say anything about writing a spy story."

"Maybe no one ever asked her," I said.

"Of course not," she said. "I would never ask such a thing."

Fortunately, I'd been gone long enough that I'd forgotten what it was that, in our family, we didn't ask.

———◆———

My grandmother was ninety-three when she died that night in January in her sleep. I wonder, as her heart slowed and failed if she dreamed of my grandfather, the half-Irish boy with the blue eyes and black hair, the one she fell in love with or, as the white light came, if she saw the frozen landscape and brilliant stars of a Russian sky.

Two days later the town newspaper ran her obituary. In that two days time, private services had been held and a private burial had occurred. Visiting hours and flowers were omitted by request. None of that was a surprise. We were private people.

As for my grandmother's literary career, if she ever wrote anything, it didn't survive. I have a few cards and notes she sent me over the years, printed carefully in old-fashioned script where the letter Ms are three straight lines crossed at the top with a bar and where the weather and best wishes figure prominently.

When I asked my uncle, who had cleaned out the house and attic after she died, if she had left any stories or notebooks, he looked surprised, "Stories? No, no stories," he said. "I did find a letter though." And he dug through a box of yellowed papers. Here is the letter she wrote and did or did not send.

Feb. 27, 1917
Colgate & Company
199 Fulton Street, New York

Dear Sir, —
Will you kindly send me a trial tube of Mirage Cream?
Yours respectfully,

Amy L. Ferris

Mirage Cream, I learned later, was advertised as "essential when one is exposed to the chilly winds and dampness of winter." At the time she wrote this letter, it would have been chilly and windy and damp in Massachusetts, and darkness would have fallen early. She had been married eight weeks, and the baby she was carrying would be dead in another six.

———◆━━━

Several years before my own mother died, she and I went to the cemetery to visit the family graves. It's easy to find my grandmother and grandfather's because we have been there so many times, but the other graves are not always easy to find, so as we walked, we talked about who was who and what she knew about them. She regretted that she didn't know anything about my father's Irish grandfather, for she was Irish herself, and she lamented that she hadn't asked more questions at the time, because, now, anyone who would have known is dead.

On that walk, I mentioned the nosegay and the baby. No, my mother didn't know of any baby Grammy would be bringing flowers to. No one had lost a baby she knew about.

After that, I spent years on and off looking for the Irish grandfather. I did find him eventually, but my mother was dead by then, and while on his path, I found the baby as well, because while people and memories die, the town keeps its records. And there in the old handwritten record book that is kept in a back room at the town hall is the baby. She is Barbara Ferris, born at home on School Street on March 29, 1917, dead nine days later of "prematurity" and "gastritis."

This date meant nothing to me. I didn't know when my grandparents married or whether Barbara was their first, middle, or last child, but I was confused about the cemetery—I had been all over it. There was no Barbara or Baby or Angel in any of our plots. So my sister Mary and I went to the family funeral parlor to see the owner. He knew our family. He was glad to see us. He reminisced. He told us, he had gone with his father to "get" my grandmother when she died. "She was a lovely woman," he said.

When I gave him Barbara's name and date of death, he turned to a wooden cabinet of small drawers and opened one. Yes, Barbara was buried in one of the family plots. As for the lack of a gravestone, he said, "Well, maybe they were too upset at the time. Maybe they thought they would do it later."

"The old families, you know," he said.

That got me to thinking about the old families. And when the microfilm viewer at the library illuminated my grandparents' newspaper marriage announcement, I knew what I wanted to know about the old families, and what had taken me decades to learn.

> A quiet wedding was solemnized at the Parish church, Wednesday evening at 6 o'clock by the pastor. The contracting parties were Miss Amy Litchfield and Mr. Oliver Morgan Ferris. Only immediate relatives of the couple attended.

A private wedding on the third of January, a Wednesday night. Not three months before their first child was born. I knew then. Barbara was my grandmother's first baby, her secret baby. A baby born at home in the old house who lived but nine days. So secret that none of her siblings knew a sister had preceded them. So secret she was laid in an unmarked grave. In a spot my grandmother knew by heart and that, one day, she showed me—a child who loved babies, and who knows now where to lay a pretty pink rose or a waxy daffodil.

Endnotes

See bibliography for full citation if not given.

Abbreviations

History (1893): *History of the Town of Hingham Massachusetts*, 1893.

Inventory (TOH): *Inventory of Historic, Architectural and Archaeological Assets*, Town of Hingham.

NAIC: Hart, Lorena Laing, Francis Hart, *Not All Is Changed: A Life History of Hingham*.

NEGHS: New England Historic Genealogical Society.

MACRIS: The Massachusetts Cultural Resource Information System.

Transactions: Transactions of the Hingham Agricultural and Horticultural Society.

Family Genealogies and Histories

Briggs: Briggs, L. Vernon, *History and genealogy of the Briggs family in Three Volumes, 1254–1937.*

Burr: *History* (1893), Vol. II.

Cushing: *History* (1893), Vol. II; Cushing, James Stevensondn, *The genealogy of the Cushing family*; Cutter, William Richard, *Genealogical and Personal Memoirs Relating to the Families of Boston and Eastern Massachusetts, Volume 2.*

Croade: *Vital records of Kingston, Massachusetts, to the year 1850; Vital Records of The Town Of Halifax Massachusetts To The End Of The Year 1849.*

Chauncey: Fowler, William Chauncey, *Memorials of the Chaunceys.*

Fuller: Abercrombie, Elizabeth, *Fuller genealogy*; Fuller, William Hyslop, *Genealogy of Some Descendants of Thomas Fuller of Woburn.*

Jones: *History* (1893), Vol. II.

Litchfield: *History* (1893), Vol. III; Litchfield, W.J., *Litchfield family in America.*

Locke: Locke, John G., *Book of the Lockes.*

Marsh: Marsh, E. J., *Genealogy of the family of George Marsh: who came from England in 1635 and settled in Hingham, Mass.*

Stowers: *History* (1893), Vol. III.

Souther: *History* (1893), Vol. III.

Tower: *History* (1893) Vol. III; Tower, Charlemagne, *Tower genealogy. An account of the descendants of John Tower, of Hingham, Mass.*

Trowbridge: *History* (1893) Vol. III; Chapman, F. W., *The Trowbridge family, or, Descendants of Thomas Trowbridge, one of the first settlers of New Haven*; Trowbridge, Francis Bacon, *The Trowbridge genealogy: history of the Trowbridge family in America.*

Chapter 1

Photo of 74 School Street courtesy of Hingham Historical Society. 1897. Note the Victorian era porch and low white fence, which stretches across the front of the house. It was removed by the 1930s.

Epigraph: Dickens, Charles, *The Life and Adventures of Martin Chuzzlewit.* London: Chapman Hall 1813. Project Gutenberg. Web. Accessed Jan. 24, 2018.

Chapter 2

Epigraph: Hawthorne, Nathaniel, *The Marble Faun: Or The Romance of Monte Beni.* Boston: Houghton, Mifflin, c1901. HathiTrust Digital Library. Web. Accessed Jan. 24, 2018.

Astrologer: Mitchell, Johanna, johannamitchell.com.

U.S. Army, "Army of the United States, Separation Qualification

Record" and "Honorable Discharge," Oliver L. Ferris, Nov. 23, 1945. Copies in possession of the author.

My parents buy a house: Notes of Oliver (Morg) Ferris in possession of the author.

Map: E.P. Dutton and Boston Map Store, "Chart of Boston Harbor and Massachusetts Bay." 1865. Norman B. Leventhal Map Center. Web. Accessed Feb. 8, 2018.

Chapter 3

Epigraph: "Military History," *History* (1893), Vol. I Pt. I, p. 284.

Col. Charles Cushing house: 74 School Street, *Inventory* (TOH), inventory no. A-1130 and MACRIS, inventory no. HIN.1130.

Paternal homestead: Jacob Cushing house, 86 Pleasant Street, *Inventory* (TOH), inventory no. A-1093 and MACRIS, inventory no. HIN.1093. According to the MACRIS Historical Narrative, in 1777, Jacob Cushing's three sons: Jacob Cushing Jr. (1742–1814), Charles Cushing (1744–1809), and Isaac Cushing (1747–1815) inherited their father's house.

"Joseph Trowbridge house was built about 1785. His house and barns were raised the same day." Burr, Fearing diary, p. 222. Note: Joseph Trowbridge was the fourth owner of the house. The land the house was built on originally belonged to Thomas Minard/Miner who, in 1636 received "a grant of land near the Training Field at Hing. Centre." *History* (1893) Vol. III, p. 71 and personal genealogies of Ruth Marsh, my great-aunt.

"most Puritan religious stamp:" Griffin, Edward M., *Old Brick: Charles Chauncy of Boston.* Note: The Chauncy family traces their descent from Charlemagne and King Alfred the Great. Fowler, William Chauncey, *Memorials of the Chaunceys.*

Thomas Croade slaves: "Capt Croade Negro womans Child named Vilot was born april the 28th 1741." "Capt Croades Negro man Named Dick Richard & his Negro woman named Flora were

Lawfully Published July: 16th: 1751." *Vital Records Of The Town Of Halifax Massachusetts To The End Of The Year 1849*, V. I, p. 65.

"Elegant" handwriting: Massachusetts Historical Society, "Notes on Halifax," *Collections of the Massachusetts Historical Society, Volume 4*, p. 282.

First five of six Croade children died as infants: Drew, Thomas Bradford, Thomas Studley Lazell, *Death records from the ancient burial ground at Kingston, Massachusetts*, p. 12. Note: Many of the children who followed also died young. *Vital Records of The Town Of Halifax Massachusetts To The End Of The Year 1849*; vital records; gravestones.

"To arms!" "To arms!" *History* (1893) Vol. 1 Pt. 1, p. 280.

The Colonel, Jacob Jr., and Isaac responded on the first day of the war: "Military History," *History* (1893), p. 277–279.

Charles Cushing: "Captain, June 22, 1775; stationed at Fort No. 2, Cambridge." Sons of the American Revolution, Massachusetts Society, *Register of Members and Records of Their Revolutionary Ancestors*, p. 112.

Charles Cushing was a Captain during Canadian Campaign. "Military History," *History* (1893), p. 283–285.

Letter excerpts this chapter: Cushing, Charles, "Letter from Charles Cushing to his brother, giving a true state of facts with regard to the Army in Canada."

"sick with fever," "the first white man:" Cunningham, George Alfred, *Cunningham's history of the town of Lunenburg: from the original grant, December 7th 1719 to January 1st, 1866*, p. 166.

"so vexed:" "Col. Cushing was a strong Republican and was so vexed by the Federalists coming into power that he left town." Burr, Fearing diary, p. 229.

Charles Cushing Probate, Worcester Co., Mass. (1809). *Probate Records. Series A, Vol. 38–39, 1809–1811*. Will: Vol. 39, p. 33–34. Inventory: Vol. 38, p. 388–390. Available on microfilm at NEGHS, Boston, Mass. (NEGHS citation.)

On July 4, 1836, Congress passed legislation that provided widows of
veterans who qualified could claim their husbands' benefits. Glasson, William Henry, *History of Military Pension Legislation in the
United States.*

Pension, "the widow," etc.: Cushing, Charles, Hannah Cushing,
Mass. (1837) number W22871. *U.S., Revolutionary War Pension
and Bounty-Land Warrant Application Files, 1800–1900.* Ancestry.
com. Web. Accessed May 5, 2017. (Original data: Revolutionary
War Pension and Bounty-Land Warrant Application Files. NARA
microfilm publication M804.)

Signed with an X: If Hannah could not write does not mean she could
not read. Girls in Colonial New England were taught to read the
Bible at a young age; writing was a separate subject, often taught
only to boys. "Women's Education in the United States," Wikipe-
dia, the Free Encyclopedia. Web. Accessed Jan. 4, 2018. (Original
data: E. Jennifer Monaghan, "Literacy Instruction and Gender in
Colonial New England," *American Quarterly* 1988 40(1): 18–41 in
JSTOR)

Photo: Abdalian, Leon H. *First Church in Hingham, Mass., "Old Ship."*
Oct. 22, 1929. Digital Commonwealth, Massachusetts Collections
online. Web. Feb. 15, 2018.

Chapter 4

Epigraph: "Agriculture," *History* (1893).Vol. I Pt. II, p. 185.

Deed of sale, Charles Cushing to Isaac Cushing (1797) Suffolk County,
"Massachusetts, Land Records, 1620–1986" *Deeds 1798–1800,*
Vol. 191–193, Vol. 192, p. 253–254. Image Number: 569–570.
FamilySearch. Web. Accessed 16 April 2014. (NEHGS citation.)

"new leaders:" *NAIC,* p. 69.

Account books, "beaver hatt," crops: Day books for Jacob and Isaac
Cushing, Journals No. 2 and 3. R. Stanton Avery Special Collections Department, Mss A 784, NEGHS.

May 7, 1827, Back Street: Hingham, Town of, *"Names of the Streets,*

Lanes, Plains, and Bridges in the Town of Hingham. Hingham: Farmer and Brown Printers. Historical pamphlet, H. Hist. M/film 76–13. Hingham Public Library.

April 27, 1877: School Street is "recognized as running from Main Street to Pleasant Street," *Index of Records of Hingham 1801–1945.* Office of Town Clerk, Town Hall, Hingham, Mass.

First Parish history: Daughters of the American Revolution, *Hingham: A Story of Its Early Settlement and Life, Its Ancient Landmarks, Its Historic Sites and Buildings,* pp. 16–26; and *NAIC.*

Inventory of estate, "set off for Mary," etc.: Isaac Cushing. Probate no. 5622 (1815). *Massachusetts, Wills and Probate Records, 1635–1991,* Plymouth County. Ancestry.com. Accessed May 12, 2017. (Original data: Massachusetts County, District and Probate Courts.)

1857 map. Village map and business directory, Massachusetts 1857. Copies for sale at the Hingham Historical Society. Original: Walling, H.F., "Map of the County of Plymouth, Massachusetts 1857."

Chapter 5

Epigraph: "Advertisement of Isaac Cushing's Real Estate." Isaac Cushing, Probate no. 5622. Ibid.

Year Without a Summer: Atkins, William Giles, *History of the town of Hawley, Franklin County, Massachusetts, from its first settlement in 1771 to 1887,* p. 86; Klingaman, William K., Nicholas P. Klingaman, *The Year Without Summer: 1816 and the Volcano that Darkened the World and Changed History;* Munger, Sean, "1816: The Mighty Operations of Nature: Societal effects of the year without a summer."

Fuller portraits: Fuller, William Hyslop, *Genealogy of Some Descendants of Thomas Fuller of Woburn.*

"a casual collection," "little sense of religion," etc.: Chazanof, William, *"Buffalo in Her Formative Years."*

Asa Fuller letter from Buffalo to his brother Azariah Fuller in Boston, Feb. 1, 1813. Fuller-Higginson Family Papers, Box 1, Folder 1,

Pocumtuck Valley Memorial Association, 10 Memorial Street, Deerfield, Mass. 01342.

"The whole Niagara frontier:" Lossing, Benson J., *Pictorial Field-book of the War of 1812.* New York: Harper & Brothers, 1868, pp. 634–55.

"great anxiety:" Asa Fuller to his brother Aaron Fuller, June 14, 1816. Fuller-Higginson Family Papers. Ibid. (This letter includes a reference to Nathan and William, Nancy Locke Fuller's brothers.)

Deed of Sale from Isaac Cushing (Jr.) to Asa Fuller, Feb. 28, 1817. Plymouth County Registry of Deeds. Book 130, p.139. Registry of Deeds Office, Plymouth, Mass. See also Deed of Sale from Asa Fuller to Joseph Trowbridge, Dec. 30, 1818. Plymouth County Registry of Deeds, Book 136, pp. 199–200. Registry of Deeds Office, Plymouth, Mass.

Asa Fuller petition "praying compensation," Jan. 20, 1819: United States Congress, *Journal of the House of Representatives of the United States, at the second session of the Fifteenth Congress, in the forty-third year of the independence of the United States.* p. 199.

Asa's petition "laid on table" Dec. 20, 1819: United States Congress, *Digested Summary and Alphabetical List of Private Claims which Have Been Presented to the House of Representatives from the First to the Thirty-first Congress.* Vol. 1, A-G, p. 680

"Asa Fuller—Innkeeper," etc.: *List of Sufferers on the Niagara Frontier from Fort Niagara to the Tonewanta Creek and from Lewiston on the Ridge Road to the widow Forsythe's.*

Nancy Fuller widow 1853: Locke, John G., *Book of the Lockes,* p. 73.

Married three times: Abercrombie, Elizabeth, *Fuller genealogy; A record of Joseph Fuller, descendant of Thomas Fuller of Woburn and Middletown, Mass.,* p. 51.

Asa's last wife: "Fuller, Asa, spouse, Curtis, Mary Jane. Wife born in 1817, baptized in 1844. His widow died in 1875. 1844 p. F50a. Fuller, Asa, died Aug 25, 1868, Sorel boarding house keeper died aged about 83. 1868 p. F40a." Simmons, Marlene, compiler, *Christ*

Church Anglican, Sorel, Quebec 1784–1899, Index to Baptisms, Marriages and Burials. Pointe Claire: Quebec Family History Society, 1999. CD.

Susanna Burr, Col. Charles Cushing, Hannah Croade Cushing, Deacon Isaac Cushing, and I are all descended from Matthew and Nazareth Cushing, the first of the Cushing family in the New World. Matthew and Nazareth and their five children came to Hingham in 1638 from England. *History* (1893) Vol. II; Cushing, James Stevensondn, *The genealogy of the Cushing family*; family vital records.

Photo of Litchfield House, 74 School Street courtesy of the Hingham Historical Society. 1889.

Chapter 6

Epigraph: *History* (1893), "Public Conveyances," Vol. I Pt. II, p. 241.

Early 1804: History offers two different timelines of Joseph's arrival in Hingham. F.E. Chapman writes on p. 60 of his genealogies that Joseph "settled in Hingham, where he married." Frances Bacon Trowbridge writes on p. 71 of his that, "Soon after his marriage he settled in Hingham, Mass."

"considerable luxury:" Trowbridge, Francis Bacon, *Trowbridge genealogy*, p. 64.

West Indies trade: "The most important family associated with the West Indies trade was Trowbridge. During the 18th and 19th century the Trowbridge family owned and commanded sloops, schooners, and the large bark "Trinidad," all employed in the West Indies trade. It is claimed that they were the largest West Indies trading concern in the United States." Foote, George, Richard Silocka, *New Haven—Maritime History and Arts.* Yale University: Yale-New Haven Teachers Institute. Web. Accessed Oct. 29, 2016.

Farmers sent sons to college: Milkofsky, Brenda, "Connecticut and the West Indies: Sugar Spurs Trans-Atlantic Trade."

"no occupation:" Dexter, Franklin Bowditch, *Biographical Sketches of the Graduates of Yale College with Annals of the College History: May 1763–July 1778.*

"reduced:" Chapman, F. W., *The Trowbridge family*, p. 52; "squandered," personal genealogies of Ruth Marsh in possession of author.

Sarah Sabin's sister: Manchester, Irving E., *The History of Colebrook*, pp. 68–72.

Joseph's youngest sister Laura married William Derbyshire of Denmark, N.Y. and Lenox Mass. in 1806 when she was 19. Joseph's brothers Hezekiah and Rosewell died in Denmark, N.Y. in Aug. and Sept. 1810. According to Denmark town clerk, the courthouse and records from that time were destroyed in a fire.

First day of Revolution: *History* (1893) Vol. I Pt. 1, p. 277, p. 280.

Revolutionary War records of Levi Burr, *U.S., Revolutionary War Pension and Bounty-Land Warrant Application Files, 1800–1900.* Ancestry.com. Web. Accessed May 2, 2009. (Original data: Revolutionary War Pension and Bounty-Land Warrant Application Files.)

Levi Burr house: 17 Leavitt St., Cape Cod, *Inventory* (TOH), inventory no. A-378 and MACRIS, inventory no. HIN.378, includes information on Burr families and history of Hingham Centre.

Education for girls: "Education," *History* (1893) Vol. I Pt. II, p. 83–154.

"snow squalls:" Murdoch, Richard K., "The Battle of Orleans, Massachusetts (1814) and Associated Events."

Petition: Joseph Trowbridge proposed new boundaries for School Street between present day Main and Spring streets. Approved March 12, 1821 by the Town. *Index of Records of Hingham 1801–1945*, p. 109. Office of Town Clerk, Town Hall, Hingham, Mass.

John Souther House, Shipcote, is located at 31 Ship Street. *Inventory* (TOH), inventory no. 1143 and MACRIS inventory no. HIN.1143. Note: Emma's husband Leavitt's shipyard was about where the yacht club is today. Daughters of the American Revolution, *Hingham: a story of its early settlement and life, its ancient landmarks, its historic sites and building*, p. 92.

"snow flakes, etc:" "Meteoric Display of 1833," Perley, Sidney, *Historic Storms of New England,* pp. 261–262.

Matthew H. Burr house, built 1841, 263 Main Street. *Inventory* (TOH), inventory no. 505 and MACRIS, inventory no. HIN.505.

"equal parts," subject to his "wife's right of dower:" Joseph Trowbridge: Probate no. 21218 (1853). *Massachusetts, Wills and Probate Records, 1635–1991.* Plymouth County, Massachusetts. Ancestry.com. Web. Accessed Aug. 19, 2017. (Original data: Massachusetts County, District and Probate Courts.)

Photo of Hingham Centre courtesy of the Bare Cove Fire Museum. 1880s–1890s.

Chapter 7

Sarahlane's name is actually Sarah Lane (Jones) Trowbridge, but I have combined her first and middle names because there are so many Sarahs in the family story, it is hard to keep them straight.

"Month of Libra," "cider presses," etc.: *New England anti-Masonic almanac for the year of Our Lord 1833.*

Roswell Jr. would have had a nickname, as his father was Roswell; I don't know it so I call him R.J. Roswell was probably a derivative of the family name Rosewell, also the name of one of Joseph's brothers.

Blacksmith shop: Deed of sale from Joseph Trowbridge to Roswell Trowbridge, May 13, 1834. Plymouth County Registry of Deeds. Book 177, p.180. Registry of Deeds Office, Plymouth, Mass.

1858 consumption deaths: Warner, Oliver, Secretary of the Commonwealth, *Report of births, marriages, and deaths in Massachusetts, for the year ending December 31,1858,* p. 73; and Shoemakers hard hit by consumption: Larkin, Jack, *The Reshaping of Everyday Life,* p. 80.

Roswell Trowbridge, liquor license: Massachusetts State Liquor Commissioner, *Annual report of the State Liquor Commissioner,* for year ending Oct. 1, 1859, p.16. And Massachusetts State Liquor Commissioner, *Annual report of the State Liquor Commissioner, for year for year ending Oct. 1, 1860*, p. 38. Google Books. Accessed June 10, 2017.

Susanna Trowbridge: Probate no. 21200. (1859.) *Massachusetts, Wills and Records, 1635–1991*. Plymouth County. Ancestry.com. Web. Accessed June 12, 2017. (Original data: Massachusetts County, District and Probate Courts.)

The majority of townsmen voted for Lincoln: *NAIC*, p. 99.

"report in Boston:" Burr, Fearing, George Lincoln, *The Town of Hingham in the Late Civil War*, p. 97.

"United States Naval Enlistment Rendezvous, 1855–1891," NARA microfilm publication M1953. Washington D.C.: National Archives and Records Administration. Henry Trowbridge, Benjamin L. Jones, George H. Merritt, Aug 1862; p. 335, V. 21. FamilySearch. Web. Accessed June 10, 2017.

"five guns," "Is his sleep less sweet," etc.: Burr, Fearing, George Lincoln, *The Town of Hingham in the Late Civil War*. Includes biographical information Benjamin Jones, pp. 312–313; Henry Trowbridge, p. 313; George Merritt pp. 388–389.

"improved as a slaughterhouse:" Burr, Fearing, diary, p. 267.

"septicemia:" Death record for Mary Ordway Trowbridge, *Massachusetts Vital Records, 1840–1911*. NEGHS. Web. Accessed May 19, 2011. (Hingham death record.)

Mary's death notice: "Trowbridge—In Hingham Centre, 1st inst, Mary Emma, wife of Henry Trowbridge, 38 years, 7 months. Her remains were carried to Newburyport for burial." *Hingham Journal*, p. 4, Feb. 16, 1883.

Hannah's brother: James E. Ferris, 26, married Nellie Sullivan, 23, on Jan. 5, 1885 in Worcester, Mass.

"Hay is being made," etc.: *Hingham Journal*, June 27, 1884.

Irishman running for mayor: "Boston Swears in First Irish-born Mayor." Mass Moments, a project of Mass Humanities. Web. Accessed Jan. 7, 2018.

Map: Beers, F. W. "Town of Hingham Plymouth County, Mass." Map. 1873. Norman B. Leventhal Map Center. Web. Accessed Feb. 8, 2018.

Chapter 8

Epigraph: "Death of Mrs. Litchfield," *Hingham Journal,* Dec. 22, 1916, p. 4.

Roswell Trowbridge: Probate 2378 (1886). Will: Vol. 168, p. 187. Plymouth Probate and Family Court, Plymouth, Mass.

"snowstorm, high winds:" Perley, Sidney, "The Winter of 1856–57," *Historic Storms of New England,* p. 323.

Lincoln ancestors: President Abraham Lincoln and I are descended from the same ancestor, Mordecai Lincoln, who is descended from Samuel Lincoln who settled in Hingham in 1637.

Memorial Resolution for Joseph H. Litchfield: *Hingham Journal,* Jan. 4, 1878.

Rozy and Wilbur at fair: Hingham Agricultural and Horticultural Society, *Transactions of the Hingham Agricultural and Horticultural Society.* See these reports: 1867–1869; 1877–1884. *Transactions* 1868: Roswell L. Litchfield, 50 cents prize for his lamb, p. 26. Pub. 1869. 1880: W.T. Litchfield, fat sheep, first prize of $1, p. 12. Pub. 1881. *Transactions* 1882: W.T. Litchfield, bantams, gratuity, 20 cents, p. 15, Pub. 1883. *Transactions* 1883: Wilbur Litchfield, black bantam chicks, gratuity 25 cents, p. 20. Other years, Rozy won for his pigs and hogs, and as he got older he judged the beef cattle, Indian corn, and poultry categories. HathiTrust Digital Library. Accessed Oct. 5, 2017.

Wilbur admission to high school: *Hingham Journal,* Friday, June 27, 1884, p. 4.

Isabel Trowbridge death notice: *Hingham Journal,* Nov. 1887. Copy in possession of author.

December 1889 weather: Davis, W.M., L. G. Schultz, et al., "Investigations of the New England Meteorological Society in the year 1889,"
Annals of Harvard College Observatory, Vol. 21, p. 111.

Photo of St. Paul's Cemetery by the author.

Chapter 9

Epigraph: "Wilbur T. Litchfield: An Appreciation," *The Brookline
Chronicle*, Brookline, Mass. May 13, 1911, p.18.

Henry's house on the corner of Union and Pleasant streets: Henry
Trowbridge House, 51 Pleasant Street, 1892. MACRIS, no.
HIN.1083 and *Inventory* (TOH), inventory no. A-1083.

Oliver Tower home: 54 School Street. Built by Joshua Higgins 1857.
Inventory (TOH), inventory no. A-1123.

Oliver Tower had many professions, as did others at that time. In
addition to being a constable and a volunteer fireman, he earned
money as a nurse and a laborer.

Number 45 School Street: "Mr. Morgan E. Ferris, son-in-law of
Mr. Oliver Tower, has recently purchased the estate of Mrs.
Melinda Sprague on School Street. The deeds were passed on
Wednesday." *Hingham Journal*, Oct. 12, 1894. See the Luther
Stephenson house: *Inventory* (TOH), inventory no. A-1117 and
MACRIS, HIN.1117.

Deed of Sale: Sarah T. Litchfield to Wilbur T. Litchfield, April 30, 1896.
Book 713, p. 421. Plymouth County Registry of Deeds. Registry of
Deeds Office, Plymouth, Mass.

Litchfield to Hingham Cooperative Bank, April 30, 1896 (recorded
May 9, 1896.) Plymouth County Registry of Deeds, Registry of
Deeds Office, Plymouth, Mass.

Litchfield, Wilbur T., Barn, "agricultural; out building; single family
dwelling" MACRIS, inventory no. HIN.1128 and *Inventory* (TOH),
inventory no. A-1128.

Boarders: Clarence M Stephenson, 21, Charles Newcomb, 45. 1900

U.S. Federal Census, Hingham, Mass., Sarah T. Litchfield, head of household.

Henry's obituary: Trowbridge, Henry. *Daily Boston Globe,* May 7, 1930.

Hannah Trowbridge's death record says she is 66; she is 78. It's probable she didn't know her birth date, as it was never reported accurately. Whether her doctor or daughter provided the date, we don't know.

Hannah T. Trowbridge: Probate no. 203297 (1935). Middlesex County Probate and Family Court, Cambridge, Mass., book 1248 p. 501. Will: book 157, p. 40. Via Massachusetts Document Retrieval online, Professional Massachusetts Public Record Researchers, Boston, Mass.

Aunt Ruth's anecdote regarding fire horses: Oral history and as told to Michael A. Shilhan for his book, *When I Think of Hingham,* p. 93.

"Twenty-five Anniversary," *Hingham Journal,* Friday, June 11, 1909, p. 4. Also an undated article, "Silver Wedding Anniversary Observed," which details gifts and attendance. Circa June 1909. Original clipping in possession of the author

Union Publishing Co., *Resident and Business Directory of Hingham and Cohasset, Massachusetts 1912–13,* Boston: Union Publishing Co, 1912. Ancestry.com. Web. Accessed Sept. 4, 2017.

Sarah T. Litchfield Probate no. 24922. Plymouth Probate and Family Court, Plymouth, Mass.

Photo courtesy Bare Cove Fire Museum.

Chapter 10

Epigraph: The entry for Senior Amy Trowbridge Litchfield in Eromdiks, the 1916 Skidmore School of Arts yearbook, p. 36. Copy provided by Skidmore College. Five years later (1922), Skidmore School of Arts became Skidmore College. (Eromdiks is Skidmore spelled backwards.)

Annie (Tower) and Morgan Ferris had three children who lived on

School Street: (1) Oliver married, had four children and lived at number 74. (2) Kathryn married, had children, and lived at number 41. (3) Gordon married, had one child, and lived at number 45. Annie and Morgan are buried in Hingham Centre Cemetery, as are their three children.

41 School Street built 1925: *Inventory* (TOH), inventory no. A-1116 and MACRIS HIN.1116.

Harvard dental school: "Hingham Centre: Ferris, Oliver Morgan, class of 1915. School St." *Quinquennial Catalogue of the Dental School of Harvard University 1869–1930.* p. 137.

"constant supervision," etc. and Skidmore School of Arts history: Lynn, Mary C., *Make No Small Plans, a History of Skidmore College.*

Village Improvement Society: *NAIC*, p. 259.

Barbara Jeanne Ferris: Born School Street, March 29, 1917. Died April 7, 1917, aged 9 days. Barbara's death notice appeared in the *Hingham Journal*, April 13, 1917.

Oliver Morgan Ferris: *U.S., World War I Draft Registration Cards, 1917–1918.* Ancestry.com. Web. (Original data: United States, Selective Service System. Washington, D.C.: National Archives and Records Administration.)

Ruth Briggs Litchfield graduated from the Training School of the New England Baptist Hospital in 1916 as a private nurse. Badger, George S. C., "Report of the Training School Committee," New England Baptist Hospital, Dec. 31, 1916, p. 16. Copy provided by New England Baptist Hospital.

Flu deaths: New England Historic Society, "The 1918 Flu Epidemic Kills Thousands in New England," NEHS. Web. Accessed Oct. 8, 1917.

"at the home of the bride's mother:" Marsh-Litchfield wedding announcement, *Hingham Journal*, June 6, 1919, p. 4.

Martha S. Skinner (Martha S. Litchfield) and her second husband Eugene F. Skinner released all interest in the house at 74 School Street because her "use has now expired." Plymouth County

Registry of Deeds. Book 1380 pp. 54–55. May 28, 1920. Registry of Deeds Office, Plymouth, Mass. Ruth L. and George F. Marsh and Amy and Oliver M. Ferris released "all right of an estate" in 74 School Street to their mother/mother-in-law Frances B. Litchfield. May 28, 1920. Plymouth County Registry of Deeds. Book 1380 pp. 55–56. Registry of Deeds Office, Plymouth, Mass.

Oliver L. Ferris enlistment record: April 20,1942 enlistment. *U.S., World War II Army Enlistment Records, 1938–1946* [database on-line]. Provo, UT, USA: Accessed Sept. 18, 2017. (Name is misspelled as Oliveo L. Ferris.); Richard Ferris enlistment record: Sept. 26, 1941 enlistment. *U.S., World War II Army Enlistment Records, 1938–1946* [database on-line]. Provo, UT, USA. Accessed Sept. 18, 2017. (Original data: National Archives and Records Administration.)

Morgan E. Ferris obituary. *Hingham Journal,* Nov. 18, 1938, p.7.

Charlotte S. Gardner attended Hanover Academy, taught school: Ford, David Barnes, *History of Hanover Academy,* pp. 95, 200. Worked as a "shoe stitcher:" Charlotte S. Gardner, 1865 Massachusetts State Census. Ancestry.com. Accessed Jan. 3, 2018.

Remembrances of Charlotte Gardner Briggs: Ruth Litchfield Marsh and Richard Ferris. Mrs. Charlotte S. Briggs obituary appeared in the *Hingham Journal,* Dec. 12, 1940.

Oliver Morgan Ferris Registration Card: *U.S., World War II Draft Registration Cards, 1942* [database on-line]. Ancestry.com. Web. Accessed Dec. 5, 2017. (Original data: *Records of the Selective Service System, 1926–1975.*)

Oliver M. Ferris obituary: *Hingham Journal,* March 25, 1965, p.3.

Property divided: Sarah F. Litchfield (also called Frances B. Litchfield): Plymouth Probate no. 105,958. See also probates of Wilbur T. Litchfield (Plymouth Probate no. 19921); Roswell Trowbridge (Plymouth Probate no. 2378); and Sarah T. Litchfield (Plymouth Probate no. 24922.)

Map: L.J. Richards, Village of Hingham, Plymouth County and Cohasset Town 1903, Massachusetts. 1903. *NAIC.*

Chapter 11

Ferris family photo.

Oliver L. Ferris married Rita Scanlan: My father became a Catholic to marry my mother, but he was only in the Church for baptisms, first communions, marriages, and funerals. He was, however, sexton of the Old Ship, the First Parish, for many years. After he died, the Minister offered a remembrance. "He was for about 30 years sexton here at Old Ship. I spoke on Sunday of how the Meetinghouse "belongs" still to all of the generations who have made it their own through their use of it and through their care of it. It certainly "belongs" too to those many sextons over the years who have had the most immediate oversight of the building. To Oliver Ferris and to all of them we give thanks." Read-Brown, Kenneth, "Musings," *Old Ship Church Newsletter,* Oct. 4, 1990.

Annie E. Ferris, Morgan's widow died in March 1948 at age 75.

Amy T. Ferris will, probate: Plymouth Probate 89P-0084-E-1. Copy in possession of author.

Epilogue

Mirage Cream: Colgate (advertisement). "What keeps the roses in our cheeks?" *The Delineator,* Vol. 94, p. 32. March 1919. New York: The Butterick Publishing Company. New York: The Butterick Publishing Company. Note: *The Delineator* was a women's magazine.

Ferris-Litchfield wedding announcement: *Hingham Journal,* Jan. 5, 1917.

About the Sources

The U.S. Federal Census is available on paid and free websites in searchable databases. The 1855 and 1865 Massachusetts State Censuses are available on various genealogy websites and at the Massachusetts State Archives, 220 Morrissey Blvd., Boston, Mass.

Vital records for the town of Hingham are available from the Town Clerk's office for a fee (Town Hall, 210 Central Street, Hingham,

MA, 02043). For other towns, contact the local town clerk. Massachusetts vital records can be ordered through the Mass.gov website for a fee. Note: Many are available online through genealogy websites, including Ancestry.com, familysearch.org, and AmericanAncestors.org. Family histories provide valuable information.

Plymouth County Probate Records, 52 Obery Street, Plymouth, Mass. Plymouth Country Registry of Deeds, 50 Obery Street, Plymouth, Mass.

U.S. Gen Web Genealogical site for the town of Hingham, Mass., the Hingham Public Library, the Hingham Historical Society, The Bare Cove Fire Museum, and the New England Historic Genealogical Society provide many historical resources for the researcher.

Bibliography

Abercrombie, Elizabeth, *Fuller genealogy; A record of Joseph Fuller, descendant of Thomas Fuller of Woburn and Middletown, Mass.* Boston: D. Clapp & Son, 1897. Internet Archive. Web. Accessed Oct. 2, 2016.

Andrews, Tamra, "Comets," *Wonders of the Sky.* Westport: Libraries Unlimited, 2004.

Atkins, William Giles, *History of the town of Hawley, Franklin County, Massachusetts, from its first settlement in 1771 to 1887.* West Cummington: the author, 1887. Internet Archive. Web. Accessed Sept. 30, 2016.

Bouvé, Thomas T. et al, *History of the Town of Hingham, Massachusetts, In Three Volumes.* Vol. I, Pts. I and II (Historical), Vol. III (Genealogical), 1893. Pub. by the Town. Cambridge: University Press. Internet Archive. Web. Accessed Jan. 9, 2018.

Briggs, L. Vernon, *History and genealogy of the Briggs family in Three Volumes, 1254–1937.* Boston: C. E. Goodspeed & Co., 1938. HathiTrust Digital Library. Web. Accessed Aug. 3, 2017.

Burnham, Robert, *Great Comets.* United Kingdom: Cambridge University Press, 2000. Google Books. Web. Accessed Oct. 2, 2017.

Burr, Fearing (1815–1896). Diary. Mr. Burr, a Hingham Centre resident, kept a journal from the time he was 25 years old until his death in 1897. Volumes are held in the Hingham Historical Society archives at 34 Main Street, Hingham, Mass.

Burr, Fearing, George Lincoln, *The Town of Hingham in the Late Civil War: With Sketches of Its Soldiers and Sailors: Also the Address and Other Exercises at the Dedication of the Soldiers' and Sailors' Monument*. Published by the Town, 1876. Internet Archive. Web. Accessed June 12, 2017.

Chapman, F. W., *The Trowbridge family, or, Descendants of Thomas Trowbridge, one of the first settlers of New Haven, Conn*. New Haven: Punderson, Crisand, 1872. Internet Archive. Web. Accessed Oct. 10, 2016.

Charlton, Peg Blackmur, *The War Years Remembered*. Hingham: Margaret F. Charlton, 1998.

Chazanof, William, *"Buffalo in Her Formative Years,"* History of Buffalo, Buffalo Architecture and History. Web. Accessed Aug. 9, 2017. (Note: reprint from a book entitled "Niagara Land: the First 200 Years," which in turn was a reprint of a series of essays published in "Sunday, the Courier Express Magazine" to celebrate the 1976 American Revolution Bicentennial.)

Clarke, Ted, *Hingham, Four Centuries of History*. Charleston: The History Press, 2011.

Cunningham, George Alfred, *Cunningham's history of the town of Lunenburg: from the original grant, December 7th 1719 to January 1st, 1866*. Lunenburg: Lunenburg Historical Society, circa 1866. Internet Archive. Web. Accessed May 5, 2017.

Cushing, Charles, "Letter from Charles Cushing to his brother, giving a true state of facts with regard to the Army in Canada," July 8, 1776. American Archives, Series 5, Volume 1, p. 128–132. Library Digital Initiatives, Northern Illinois University. Web. Accessed Aug. 5, 2017.

Cushing, James Stevensondn, *The genealogy of the Cushing family, an account of the ancestors and descendants of Matthew Cushing, who came to America in 1638*. Montreal: The Perrault printing Co., 1905. © BiblioBazaar, LLC.

Cutter, William Richard, *Genealogical and Personal Memoirs Relating to the Families of Boston and Eastern Massachusetts, Volume 2.* Boston: Lewis Historical Publishing Company, 1908. Google Books. Web. Accessed Jan. 5, 2018.

Daughters of the American Revolution, *Hingham: a story of its early settlement and life, its ancient landmarks, its historic sites and building.* Hingham: Old Colony Chapter, 1911. Internet Archive. Web. Accessed Jan. 3, 2018.

Davis, W.M., Schultz, L. G, et al., "Investigations of the New England Meteorological Society in the year 1889," *Annals of Harvard College Observatory,* Vol. 21, pp.105–274. Cambridge: William H. Wheeler, 1890. SAO/NASA Astrophysics Data System. Web. Accessed May 30, 2017.

Delineator, The, March 1919, Vol. 94. New York: The Butterick Publishing Company. Google Books. Web. Accessed Sept. 21, 2017.

Dexter, Franklin Bowditch, *Biographical Sketches of the Graduates of Yale College with Annals of the College History: May 1763–July 1778,* Vol. III. New York: Henry Holt and Co., 1903. Google Books. Web. Accessed Aug. 3, 2017.

Diner, Hasia A., *Erin's Daughters in America: Irish Immigrant Women in the Nineteenth Century.* Baltimore: John Hopkins University Press, 1983.

Drew, Thomas Bradford, Thomas Studley Lazell, *Death records from the ancient burial ground at Kingston, Massachusetts.* Boston: Massachusetts Society of Mayflower Descendants, 1905, Internet Archive. Web. Accessed Aug. 1, 2017.

Ferling, John, *Independence, The Struggle to set America Free.* New York: Bloomsbury Press, 2011.

Fixico, Donald, "A Native Nations Perspective on the War of 1812," War of 1812. Public Broadcasting Service. Web. Accessed Aug. 14, 2017.

Foley, Mason, *Hingham Old and New.* Hingham: Hingham Tercentenary Committee, 1935.

Foote, George, Richard Silocka, *New Haven—Maritime History and Arts.* Yale University: Yale-New Haven Teachers Institute. Web. Accessed Oct. 29, 2016.

Ford, David B., *History of Hanover Academy.* Boston: H.M. Hight, Printer, 1899. HathiTrust Digital Library. Web. Accessed Jan. 15, 2018.

Foster, Gerald, *American Houses, A field guide to the architecture of the home.* Boston: Houghton Mifflin Company, 2004.

Fowler, William Chauncey, *Memorials of the Chaunceys: including President Chauncy, his ancestors and descendants.* Boston: H.W. Dutton and son, 1858. Internet Archive. Web. Accessed August 3, 2017.

Fuller, William Hyslop, *Genealogy of Some Descendants of Thomas Fuller of Woburn.* Palmer: C.B. Fiske & Co., 1919. Internet Archive. Web. Accessed Aug. 9, 2017.

Gallman, J. Matthew, editor, *The Civil War Chronicle, The Only Day-by-Day Portrait of America's Tragic Conflict as Told by Soldiers, Journalists, Politicians, Farmers, Nurses, Slaves, and Other Eyewitnesses.* New York: Crown Publishers, 2000.

Glasson, William Henry, *History of Military Pension Legislation in the United States.* New York: Columbia University, 1900. Google Books. Web. Accessed Sept. 22, 2017.

Griffin, Edward M., *Old Brick: Charles Chauncy of Boston.* Minneapolis: University of Minnesota Press, 1980.

Halifax, Town of, *Vital Records Of The Town Of Halifax Massachusetts To The End Of The Year 1849.* Boston: Massachusetts Society of Mayflower Descendants, 1905. Internet Archive. Web. Accessed May 5, 2017.

Hart, Lorena Laing, Francis Russell Hart, *Not all is Changed, A Life History of Hingham.* Hingham: The Hingham Historical Commission, 1993.

Hazard, Blanche Evans, *The organization of the boot and shoe industry in Massachusetts before 1875.* Cambridge: Harvard

University Press, 1921. Internet Archive. Web. Accessed June 11, 2017.

Hingham Agricultural and Horticultural Society, *Transactions of the Hingham Agricultural and Horticultural Society.* Pub. by the Society. 1858–61, 1867–69,1870–76, and 1877–84 annual reports are online at HathiTrust Digital Library. Web. Accessed Aug. 2, 2017.

Hingham Historical Commission, *Inventory of Historic, Architectural and Archaeological Assets* online. Town of Hingham. Web. Accessed Jan. 5, 2018.

Hingham, Town of, *"Names of the Streets, Lanes, Plains, and Bridges in the Town of Hingham,* Hingham: Farmer and Brown Printers. Historical pamphlet, H. Hist. M/film 76-13. Hingham Public Library.

Howland, Esther Allen, *The New England Economical Housekeeper, and Family Receipt Book.* Cincinnati: H.W. Derby, 1845. "Feeding America: The Historic American Cookbook Project." East Lansing: Michigan State University Libraries. Web. Accessed Aug. 9, 2017.

Kingston, Town of, *Vital records of Kingston, Massachusetts, to the year 1850.* Boston: NEGHS, 1911. Internet Archive. Web. Accessed May 5, 2017.

Klingaman, William K., Nicholas P. Klingaman, *The Year Without Summer: 1816 and the Volcano that Darkened the World and Changed History.* New York: St. Martin's Press, 2013.

Kronk, Gary W., "November meteor showers," *Meteor Showers: An Annotated Catalog.* New York: Springer Science & Business Media, 1988, 2014. Google Books. Web. Accessed Oct. 30, 2016.

Lakin, Jack, *The Reshaping of Everyday Life, 1790–1840.* New York: Harper & Row, 1988.

Larkin, Jack, *Where We Worked: A Celebration Of America's Workers And The Nation They Built.* Guilford: Lyons Press, 2010.

Lewis, Meriwether, William Clark, *The Journals of the Lewis and Clark Expedition Online*. Center for Digital Research in the Humanities in partnership with the University of Nebraska Press and the National Endowment for the Humanities. Web. Accessed Oct. 28, 2016.

Lincoln, Calvin, *A Discourse Delivered to the First Parish in Hingham, September 8, 1869: On Re-opening Their Meeting-house*. Hingham: The Parish, 1873. Google Books. Web. Accessed Sept. 4, 2017.

Lincoln, Solomon, *An address delivered before the citizens of the town of Hingham on the twenty-eighth of September, 1835: being the two hundredth anniversary of the settlement of the town*. Hingham: J. Farmer, 1835. Internet Archive. Web. Accessed Jan. 5, 2018.

Lincoln, Solomon, Jr., *History of Hingham, Plymouth County, Massachusetts*. Hingham: Gill, Farmer & Brown, 1827. Google Books. Web. Accessed Aug. 12, 2017.

List of Sufferers on the Niagara Frontier from Fort Niagara to the Tonewanta Creek and from Lewiston on the Ridge Road to the widow Forsythe's. 1814. Buffalo History Museum, New York Heritage Digital Collections. Web. Accessed May 16, 2017.

Litchfield, W.J., *Litchfield family in America*. Southbridge: W.J. Litchfield, 1901. Internet Archive. Web. Accessed Jan. 10, 2017.

Locke, John G., *Book of the Lockes*. Boston: J. Munroe and Co., 1853. Internet Archive. Web. Accessed Oct. 5, 2016.

Lossing, Benson J, *Pictorial Field-book of the War of 1812*. New York: Harper & Brothers, 1868. Internet Archive. Web. Accessed Oct. 1, 2016.

Loveland, Sterling Nye, *Quinquennial Catalogue of the Dental School of Harvard University 1869–1930*, p. 137. Cambridge: The Harvard University Press, 1933. Internet Archive. Web. Accessed Sept. 2, 2017.

Lynch-Brennan, Margaret, *The Irish Bridget: Irish Immigrant*

Women in Domestic Service in America, 1840–1930. New York: Syracuse University Press, 2009.

Lynn, Mary C., *Make No Small Plans, A History of Skidmore College.* Sarasota Springs: Skidmore College, 2000.

Manchester, Irving E., *The History of Colebrook.* Winsted: The Citizen Printing Company, 1935. Internet Archive. Web. Accessed Jan. 3, 2018.

Marsh, E. J., *Genealogy of the family of George Marsh: who came from England in 1635 and settled in Hingham, Mass.* Leominster: Press of F.N. Boutwell, 1887. Internet Archive. Web. Accessed Aug. 2, 2017.

Massachusetts Historical Commission, "Massachusetts Cultural Resource Information System online" (MACRIS). Web. Accessed Jan. 5, 2018.

Massachusetts Historical Society, "Notes on Halifax," *Collections of the Massachusetts Historical Society, Volume 4.* Boston: The Society, 1846. Google Books. Web. Accessed Aug. 1, 2017.

Massachusetts State Liquor Commissioner, *Annual report of the State Liquor Commissioner, for year ending Oct. 1, 1859.* Boston: William White, Printer to the State, 1859. Google Books. Web. Accessed June 10, 2017.

Massachusetts State Liquor Commissioner, *Annual report of the State Liquor Commissioner, for year ending Oct. 1, 1860.* Boston: William White, Printer to the State, 1860. Google Books. Web. Accessed June 10, 2017.

Milkofsky, Brenda, "Connecticut and the West Indies: Sugar Spurs Trans-Atlantic Trade." Connecticuthistory.org, Connecticut Humanities. Web. Accessed Jan. 24, 2018.

Munger, Sean, "1816: The Mighty Operations of Nature: Societal effects of the year without a summer." *Madison Historical Review*: Vol. 10, Article 3, 2013. Web. Accessed Sept. 30, 2016.

Murdoch, Richard K., "The Battle of Orleans, Massachusetts

(1814) and Associated Events," *The American Neptune* 24 (July 1964), pp. 172–182.

New England anti-Masonic almanac for the year of Our Lord 1833. Boston: John Marsh & Co., 1831. Internet Archive. Web. Accessed June 10, 2017.

New England Historical Society, "The 1918 Flu Epidemic Kills Thousands in New England." New England Historical Society, 2017. Web. Accessed Oct. 8, 1917.

Perley, Sidney, *Historic Storms of New England: Its Gales, Hurricanes, Tornadoes, Showers with Thunder and Lightning, Great Snow Storms, Rains, Freshets, Floods, Droughts, Cold Winters, Hot Summers, Avalanches, Earthquakes, Dark Days, Comets, Aurora-borealis, Phenomena in the Heavens, Wrecks Along the Coast, with Incidents and Anecdotes, Amusing and Pathetic.* Salem: Salem Press Publishing and Printing Company, 1891. Google Books. Web. Accessed June 12, 2017.

Premo, Terri L., *Winter Friends, Women Growing Old in the New Republic, 1785–1835*. Urbana: University of Illinois Press, 1990.

Renick, Barbara, *Genealogy 101: How to Trace Your Family's History and Heritage.* Nashville: Rutledge Hill Press, 2003.

Robinson, Donald F., *Two Hundred Years in South Hingham, 1746–1946*. Hingham: Hingham Historical Society, 1980.

Schlesinger, Arthur M. Jr., *Almanac of American History.* New York: Barnes and Noble Books, 1993.

Shilhan, Michael J., *When I Think of Hingham.* Hingham: Hingham Historical Society and Hingham Historical Commission, 1976.

Sons of the American Revolution. Massachusetts Society, *Register of Members and Records of Their Revolutionary Ancestors.* Pub: The Society, 1913. Google Books. Web. Accessed Jan. 20, 2018.

Tower, Charlemagne, *Tower genealogy. An account of the descendants of John Tower, of Hingham, Mass.* Cambridge: John

Wilson & Son, 1891. Internet Archive. Web. Accessed Oct. 2, 2017.

Tower Genealogical Society, *The Annual Reports of the Tower Genealogical Society for the years 1922, 23, 24, 25*. Boston: Tower Genealogical Society, Dec. 31, 1925. Internet Archive. Web. Accessed Oct. 8, 2017.

Trowbridge, Francis Bacon, *The Trowbridge Genealogy: History of the Trowbridge Family In America*. New Haven: Printed for the compiler, 1908. Internet Archive. Web. Accessed May 17, 2017.

Union Publishing Co., *Resident and Business Directory of Hingham and Cohasset, Massachusetts 1912–13*, Boston: Union Publishing Co, 1912. Ancestry.com. Web. Accessed Sept. 4, 2017.

United States Congress, *Journal of the House of Representatives of the United States, at the second session of the Fifteenth Congress, in the forty-third year of the independence of the United States.* Washington: U.S. Government Printing Office, 1818 [1819]. Google Books. Web. Accessed Aug. 16, 2017.

United States Congress, *Digested Summary and Alphabetical List of Private Claims which Have Been Presented to the House of Representatives from the First to the Thirty-first Congress.* Vol. 1, A-G, p. 680. Washington, D.C.: Wm. M. Belt, 1853. Google Books. Web. Accessed Oct. 1, 2016.

Warner, Oliver, Secretary of the Commonwealth, *Report of births, marriages, and deaths in Massachusetts, for the year ending December 31, 1858*, p. 73. Boston: William White, 1859. Google Books. Web. Accessed Nov. 17, 2016.

Thanks

Thank you to those who have gone but left some of their stories: Richard Ferris Sr., Ruth Litchfield Marsh, and my parents, Rita and Morg Ferris. Thanks to Elaine and John Ferris for their help and hospitality when my search for story took me to Ireland.

Thank you to the staffs at the Hingham Historical Society, the Hingham Public Library, the Hingham Town Clerk's office, and the Bare Cove Fire Museum for research assistance.

Additional thanks to Genealogist Lilly Cleveland for her work and to Mary and Peter Gens, who did so much land and probate research.

I am grateful to all the friends and writers who read or listened to my stories, including Gena Corea, Peg Cross, Diana Kightlinger, Sher Davidson, Joan Johnson, Ann Conley, Nancy Spohn, Delayne Giardini, Susan Chatard, Debra Warren, Ann Snyder, Alexa Timchuk, Mazie Manley, Kathy Munsel, Brenda Lobbato, Barbara Kelley, A. M. O'Malley, and Grant Miller. And to the Portland Community College teachers and students who helped me decide how to tell this story, I appreciate your time and attention.

Thank you to my sisters Ann, Judy, Susan, Mary, Amy and Ellen and their families and to Richard Ferris Jr. and to all of my cousins in all their degrees.

Thank you to my children Renee, Carey, and Chris and their families. And to my grandchildren Alexa, Austin, Molly, Madisen, Paige, Max, and Danielle who listened to these stories for years and who only occasionally said, "You already told us that."

The Hingham Centre baseball team. Back row left to right: Bill Shedd, Henry Ripley, Fred Lane, Frank Reed, Wilbur Litchfield, Harry Shedd. Photo courtesy Bare Cove Fire Museum: Kimball family photo. Circa 1882.

Roswell (Rozy) Lincoln Litchfield, Chief District Engineer. 1890s. Family photo.

Martha Sprague Litchfield. 1890s. Family photo.

Wilbur Litchfield, Superintendent of
Fire Alarms. 1890s. Family photo.

Frances Briggs Litchfield, age 21. 1892. Family photo.

Charlotte Gardner Briggs, right, in front of the
Briggs family home in Norwell. Family photo.

Ruth, left, and Amy Litchfield with their maternal
grandfather William Briggs. Circa 1897. Family photo.

Amy Trowbridge Litchfield, age 17. 1912. Family photo.

Ruth Briggs Litchfield, age 19. 1912. Family photo.

Rozy Litchfield and Prince in front of his meat market at 112 Main Street in the Centre. Circa 1900. Photo courtesy of the Hingham Historical Society.

Tower-Ferris family, three generations: Front row from left: Morgan Ferris, 62; Oliver Tower, 72; Morg (Oliver) Ferris, 3; Ann Tower, 72; Annie Tower Ferris, 48. Back row from left: Kathryn Ferris, 20, Marjorie Ferris, 2; Oliver Morgan Ferris, 27; Amy Litchfield Ferris, 26; Richard Ferris; 7 months, Gordon Ferris, 14. Taken at the Tower home at 54 School Street. 1921. Family photo.

Three generations of matriarchs. From left:
Charlotte Gardner Briggs, 95, Amy Litchfield
Ferris, 42, Frances Briggs Litchfield, 66.
Circa 1937. School Street parlor. Family photo.

Rita and Morg (Oliver) Ferris in front of the
house on School Street. 1942. Family photo.

Made in the USA
Columbia, SC
01 June 2019